Rip, Strip, & Row!
A Builder's Guide to the Cosine Wherry

by J.D. Brown

Designer: John Hartsock

Developer: Bob & Erica Pickett

FLOUNDER BAY BOAT LUMBER
Third & "O" Streets
Anacortes, Washington 98221
(206) 293-2369

TAMAL VISTA PUBLICATIONS
222 Madrone Avenue
Larkspur, California 94939

This book represents the fine efforts of many people.

Bob and Erica Pickett of Flounder Bay Boat Lumber provided years of boatbuilding experience, hours of labor, and their best materials for the prototype. Most of all they had an unfaltering faith that it was possible to design and build a truly superior rowboat.

John Hartsock put together his love of boats and considerable expertise as an engineer to produce the exquisite design of the Cosine Wherry.

Virginia Hartsock spent a week's vacation rowing the waters of Puget Sound and the San Juan Islands to confirm that her husband's design was, indeed, the best.

Margaret Backenheimer came through as editor when it was most needed.

Wayne deFremery did the lettering for the drawings and serves as an example of what youth can bring to a project when given the opportunity.

Warren and Joan Young lent their skills and patience to the photographic and layout work.

Marty Loken did the wonderful cover photo.

And the utmost thanks goes to our publisher, Kathi deFremery, whose belief in this project, combined with her hard work and coordinating genius, kept everyone afloat until the book was safely into harbor.

Second Edition
Copyright © 1985 J.D. Brown

Tamal Vista Publications

ISBN: 0-917436-02-4
Library of Congress Catalog Card Number: 85- 51141

Dedication

This book represents the cooperative efforts of many people with many talents. It is dedicated, in turn, to all who have the courage to seek out their own talents and who find the grace to share those talents with others.

Table of Contents

I. INTRODUCTION 3

II. THE MOLD 9

III. PLANKING THE HULL 25

IV. FIBERGLASSING THE HULL 37

V. FIBERGLASSING THE INTERIOR 45

VI. THE INSIDE FINISH 53

VII. TRANSPORT 67

VIII. ROWING 69

IX. FOOTNOTES ON MATERIALS 71

X. MATERIALS LIST 75

XI. DESIGN DETAILS 77

XII. GLOSSARY 79

XIII. AN UPDATE FROM THE BUILDER 81

What's a Cosine Wherry?

The Cosine Wherry is a strong, lightweight, beautiful, high performance 14-foot rowboat, the newest design by John Hartsock of Edmonds, Washington. Combining years of rowing experience with his knowledge of computerized hull designs, Mr. Hartsock has created a single rowboat to satisfy the various recreational requirements of a family, the practical demands of the sportsman, and the competitive desires of the serious rower. Few designs even attempt to combine light weight and high performance with stability, comfort, and rugged durability. Usually a rowboat capable of toting a heavy load is itself too heavy to row easily. By the same token, a rowboat which rows like a dream and cartops like a feather is usually too fragile to trust with extra pasengers or risk in rough seas. The Cosine Wherry, however, offers the best of both worlds: it's light, fast, and a joy to row, yet tough, stable, and capable of hauling plenty of passengers and gear.

The Cosine Wherry is the result of years of development and testing, the fourth generation in a series of special cosine designs. *Cosine* refers to the mathematical methods Mr. Hartsock used to generate the design. The traditional way to create a new boat is to draw a set of lines and adjust them on paper until they "look right" to the designer. The technical elements and calculations are then modified to fit these lines. In creating the Cosine Wherry, however, Mr. Hartsock reversed the traditional sequence. He calculated the optimum performance and shapes first, expressing them as mathematical equations; only then, with the aid of a computer, did he draw the lines of the boat to conform with his calculations. The advantage was that Mr. Hartsock did not have to alter a single element of his design at the expense of another element. The design of the Cosine Wherry is therefore a computer-perfect integration of each basic element.

Designing a boat, however, is as much a matter of personal expertise as mathematical theory. Computers help, but good designs still come from direct experience. Mr. Hartsock not only studied the lines of classic rowing craft, but he also put those boats to the test on the water. He compared the performance of each boat against other boats of similar design in a variety of sea conditions, and then translated his conclusions into a set of ideal design equations. In effect, the Cosine Wherry is an exquisite blend of old world thought and design with new world materials and technology.

The success of a new design, no matter how mathematically sophisticated, is in the actual performance. Several new Cosines are already on the water, built in the past few months by independent rowers (some of whom were previously inexperienced boat builders). They report that their boats have proven themselves in calm lakes, choppy inlets, wide harbors, and narrow rivers. A few effortless strokes pull the boat up to hull speed, and it then tracks through the water like a laser beam. It is particularly quick when two people take a pull on the oars. The full and gradual bilges make for a comfortable ride, keeping everyone dry when the waves and swells act up. A fairly high stern sees to it that the Cosine Wherry maintains its balance even in a stiff crosswind. The wood strip construction means this boat weights in at less than a hundred pounds, light enough to cartop. In short, the Cosine Wherry lives up to its numbers.

We can't absolutely guarantee you a blue ribbon at next year's rowing regatta—nor do we advise you to make a transoceanic passage in this rowboat—but we can promise that you will appreciate its fine design, its beauty, and its versatility. Above all, we predict you'll rediscover, or discover for the first time, the profound pleasure of rowing with a Cosine Wherry.

What's a Stripper?

The term stripper has several interesting meanings, but in fine boatbuilding it refers to an easy, increasingly popular way to build beautiful wooden boats. Thin strips of wood are laid over a mold, edge glued in position, fiberglassed, then removed from the mold. This produces a ribless boat which is extremely lightweight, but incredibly strong.

The home boatbuilder will have no trouble mastering the methods of wood strip construction. No sophisticated tools or materials are needed; no extensive woodworking skills are required. You can build a laminated wood-strip fiberglass boat in a one-car garage, a basement, or the backyard. The result is a handmade boat with sleek lines, the warm glow of natural wood, and a fiberglass coating which will reduce yearly maintenance to almost zero.

What's the catch?

Well, it does take patience. But if you have that, you can build a boat superior to any you could buy.

About the Authors

BOB and ERICA PICKETT are proprietors of an internationally-renowned marine lumber company located in Anacortes, Washington, the gateway to the San Juan Islands in Puget Sound. The Picketts are among a handful of dealers anywhere in the world who cannot only sell customers the best wood for a boat but tell them exactly how to install each piece. Erica Pickett, a native of the Ballard shipbuilding district of Seattle, is an expert in marine paints and finishes. Bob Pickett has rowed and sailed ever since his youth in Tampa Bay, a good portion of which he spent tending a 21-foot knockabout sloop. Since establishing Flounder Bay Boat Lumber in 1971, the Picketts have built and helped others build a wide range of seaworthy craft. It was in their shop that they perfected the strip construction techniques described in this book. The Cosine Wherry is the latest project in the Picketts' commitment to the great traditions of fine wood boat building in America.

JOHN HARTSOCK is a consulting engineer based in the Northwest. An avid rower and author, he has created a series of computer-assisted boat designs. He builds the boats he designs and tests them himself on the lakes, rivers, and harbors around Puget Sound. The 14-foot Cosine Wherry is his most advanced and popular design.

J.D. BROWN is author of *DIGGING TO CHINA* (Soho Press, 1991). He writes about travel and the outdoors for *AMERICAN HEALTH, THE BOSTON GLOBE, THE CHICAGO TRIBUNE, CHEVRON USA ODYSSEY, THE CHRISTIAN SCIENCE MONITOR, NEWSDAY, THE WASHINGTON POST,* and the *WALL STREET JOURNAL GUIDES TO BUSINESS TRAVEL (Fodor's).* In 1984 he was a visiting professor at a medical college in China. He continues to travel frequently throughout the Orient.

To Build or Not to Build?

That's a serious question. Perhaps you've never built a boat before—not even the sort that floats in the bathtub. It makes no difference. Strip building a Cosine Wherry requires no previous experience, no special woodworking skills. In fact, if you can drive a nail, saw a board, and point a glue gun, you can assemble this boat.

All you really need are thorough, step-by-step instructions, sturdy marine materials, and plenty of patience. We supply everything but the patience.

It takes some 220 hours for the first-time boatbuilder. That adds up to a few pounds of dedication on your part; but if you decide to give it a go, then read this book through, use good materials, take your time, and the work will sail by. Before you know it, you'll have a stunning rowboat requiring little maintenance. It will row as only a real rowboat can. Best of all, you'll have the deep satisfaction of having built it yourself.

Before You Begin

It's important that you read the entire book before beginning to build. A complete understanding of the project will make each step along the way a great deal more understandable, and will probably save a lot of errors. Be sure to pay attention to the recommendations on materials in the last chapter. Remember, you're going to put a lot of hours into building this boat, and the boat is one that can last a lifetime, so select your materials carefully. If you run into trouble, need additional information, have trouble locating proper materials, or just need some moral support, give us a call at FLOUNDER BAY BOAT LUMBER in Anacortes, Washington. (206) 293-2369

A Quick Overview

If you've never built a small boat from a mold before, it helps to have the overall picture in mind. Here we give you an overview in six quick pictures—and in the pages that follow, we will fill you in on all the details, step-by-step.

From the full size patterns you cut out the mold pieces and assemble them.

Then, strip by strip you assemble the hull over the mold . . .

. . . and fiberglass the outside.

Next, you flip the boat over to scrape, sand and fiberglass the inside.

After you've added some finishing touches to the inside, you take your boat to the water . . .

. . . and row away!   It's that simple . . . almost . . .

The mold is a temporary skeleton on which you build the boat hull. It's a manikin, but instead of draping it in cloth, you will be clothing it in cedar planks and fiberglass.

Once assembled, this boat mold resembles a 16-foot turkey carcass picked clean. The spine of this turkey is called the strongback; the ribs are called stations. The strongback is a straight wooden platform on sawhorses; the stations are forms attached to the strongback and they give you the exact shape of the hull. Study the diagram of the mold. This is what you have to build first, complete with cleats and gussets for bracing each station. You may want to refer back to this drawing if you forget what some part of this beast is called.

Everything depends on building an accurate mold. It gives the essential form, for better or worse, to the finished boat. So the more care you take with the mold, the better.

Mold-building is not (repeat: not) the most exciting phase of small boat construction. We have not been able to find a single boat-builder who would rank it ahead of a week's cruise in the Florida Keys. Building a mold even ranks slightly below painting a picket fence. Nevertheless, you can't build a decent rowboat without a mold, so this is where everyone must start. Actually, mold assembly is very simple. The problem is, it is also extremely tedious. There are lots of little steps (which must be why boat molds are often called jigs) and you have to be fussy and finicky about lining everything up. But when you take some time and do it right, you can tell yourself, at least, that planking the hull will be a smooth, satisfying operation.

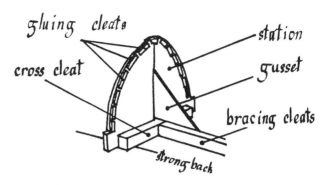

Typical station mold and associated parts.

Materials for Mold Assembly

All wood should be straight and kiln dried.

2 - 2x6, 16' long for strongback
3 sheets of ⅝" thick particle board for stations
About 16' of 2x2 lumber for station cleats
About 14' of 1x1 lumber strips for glue cleats
2 - 2x4s for plumb sticks
2 sawhorses (or scrap lumber to build a strongback support)
An assortment of 1" finish nails, 1" duplex nails, and longer nails to attach cleats to strongback
Several dozen #14, 3" wood screws
Plenty of 1½" and 2" wood screws to secure other parts of the beast
2 six-packs of your favorite beverage (more if necessary)
1 half sheet of ½" thick marine plywood

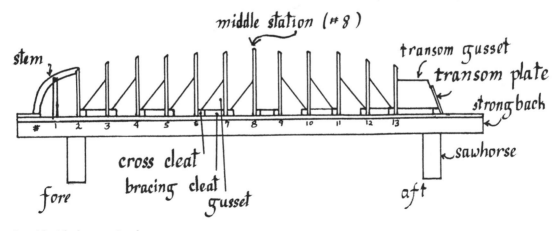

Completed mold with the stem in place.

Tools you will need, beginning at the bottom center and going clockwise: rasp, hand plane, surform, longboard for sanding, speed block sander, jig saw, glue gun and glue sticks, spring clamps, squeegee.

Tools for Mold Assembly

Tools do not have to be straight or dry, but it sure helps!

Hammer	Level	Straight-edge
Large square	Pencil	Pen
Jig-saw	Hand saw	Pins (push pins
Spoke shave	Block plane	or sewing)
Strapping tape (lots)	Wood glue	Surform
Chalk line (optional)		Utility knife

CLAMPS—the more the better. Since you'll need spring clamps later to plank the hull, you might as well get a hold of some now. How many? Nineteen would be great; the minimum is eight.

The Strongback

Construct your strongback of two kiln-dried 2"x6" 16' boards. To live up to its name, the strongback must be strong, straight and true. Don't be tempted by low-priced green or warped lumber.

Screw the two boards together, the edge of one board running along the center of the face of the other board in a short, wide "T" shape. We found that #14 3" wood screws worked out perfectly.

Set in screws every 12" the length of the strongback. Alternate them slightly left and right of center so that you can later draw a centerline the full length of the strongback.

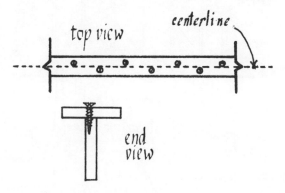

Fastening pattern for the strongback assembly.

Sawhorses

We supported our strongback on two sawhorses. The sawhorses were short, about 24″ high. They don't need to be any higher than that, unless you're eight-feet tall. By the time you add stations to the strongback (ribs to the turkey spine) you'll be at a comfortable working height.

The sawhorses must be planted securely to terra firma. In fact, we nailed the sawhorse legs to the workshop floor. This prevented the legs from twisting out of line as we built the rest of the mold. If you're working on a concrete floor or in the backyard, improvise. Your goal is support stability for the mold.

Once your sawhorses or other supports are entrenched, lay the strongback astraddle. Check to see if the strongback is resting level. Place your level lengthwise and crosswise in several places on the strongback. If you don't get level readings, slip wood shims under the strongback until you do. Then nail or screw your strongback to its platforms.

Strongback Centerline

The strongback centerline is the first of many useful reference lines you'll need to lay out your mold. Strike a straight line the full length of the strongback in the exact center. A chalk line will give you a straight line.

So will a string nailed at the center of each end of the strongback. Ink in the line with a straight-edge or straight batten of wood.

Side view of the strongback with the centerline inked in.

Plumb Sticks

An extremely handy system of reference lines in space is provided by a set of trusty plumb sticks. Plumb sticks are erected at the stem and stern of boat molds, and strings are stretched between sticks to check for keel line, waterlines and sheerline. We found such lines indispensable as we assembled our mold and planked the boat hull.

We used two 2x4s, dry and straight, for our plumb sticks. After we fastened each 2x4 to the rafters and the floor, we checked an edge and a face on each with our level to assure plumbness. One plumb stick was set directly on line with the strongback centerline at the stem; the other on the same line at the stern.

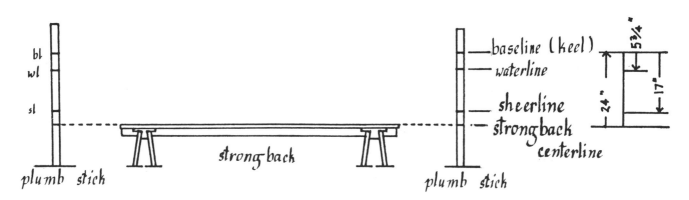

The plumb sticks are used to check the alignment of the stations on the strongback.

You may have to improvise to come up with your own version of plumb sticks. (Sometimes you can attach plumb sticks to the ends of the strongback, for example, making sure that the strongback is longer than the boat mold so the plumb sticks won't interfere.)

Once you've centered and secured your plumb sticks, mark some handy reference points. First project the centerline onto the plumb stick by measuring across on the level from the strongback to the plumb stick (see diagram). Mark this point on each plumb stick. From this mark, measure exactly 24″ up the plumb sticks. Label this second mark your baseline. (The baseline is where the keel of your boat will be—the bottom line, so to speak.) Now from the baseline, measure down 5¾″ and mark this point the waterline. (This is the line at which the boat sits in the water.) Go back up to the baseline, the highest line on the plumb stick, and measure down 17″. Label this point the sheerpoint. (The sheer connects the first plank to the stem and transom.)

Tie a tight string from baseline to baseline; check the string with a level. This line will make it a breeze to center each station on the strongback.

Plumb stick with a string tied at the baseline mark.

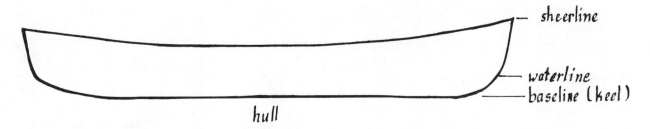

sheerline

waterline
baseline (keel)

hull

When the hull is completed, this is where the plumb stick lines will fall.

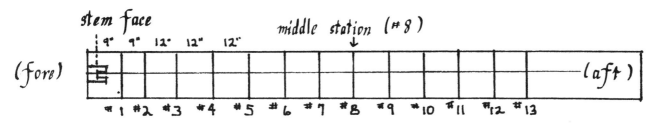

Positioning of the stations on the strongback.

Station Cross-Lines

Your strongback has its centerline, but where do you place each station? They go crosswise on the spine, so you need to draw in a cross line for each station.

Measure the exact length of your strongback. (It's sixteen foot lumber, but is it a true 16' long?) Divide by 2 and mark the exact center of the strongback length. Then, use a square to draw a line across the centerline of the strongback at this exact mid-point. This cross line tells you where to place the middle station of the mold.

Since each station is 9″ or 12″ apart, you can now measure off a total of 14 intervals fore and aft of the mid station cross line. (You end up with what looks like a schematic drawing of a giant autoharp.)

The stations are numbered in order starting at the stem. The middle station is #8. If you haven't decided which end is which on your strongback, do so now.

Cut Stations

The boat plans have a pattern for each station. You need to trace that pattern onto ⅛″ thick particle board and cut out each station with a jigsaw.

We used the "pin punch" method to trace station patterns onto particle board sheets. Securely tape the station pattern to the board and then punch along the pattern lines at 2″ or 3″ intervals. Remove the punched pattern. (Sewing pins, push pins, or small finishing nails will work as punches.)

At each punch in the wood, we inserted a small finishing nail. We used a flexible batten of wood as a guide for penciling in the pattern lines.

Trace the station patterns onto your sheet of wood. Cut out each station, use sand paper or a small block plane to smooth the edge.

Now use a plane, spokeshave, or surform to cut a rough bevel. Angle almost down to your inside bevel line, but don't cut a full bevel—you may want some room to play later.

The reason for a bevel on the curved edges of the stations will be obvious once you plank the hull. Since the planks have to bend around the stations, the bevel allows them to flow smoothly from station to station. (No ugly bulges along the way.)

Finally, use a large square to draw a centerline on the back (unbeveled side) of each station.

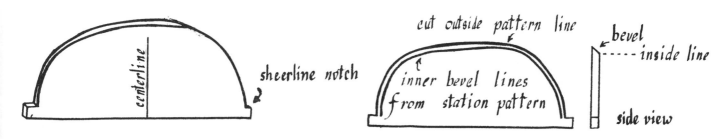

Typical station shape, showing bevel line, sheerline notch, and centerline.

Cross Cleats

The stations you cut will be placed under extreme force when you plank the hull, so they must be attached securely to the strongback. Otherwise the ribs of our spine-like mold will bend out of position and the hull will resemble a crumpled hot tub.

Attach the stations to the strongback with cleats. Cleats are nothing fancier than 2″x2″ sticks of wood fastened crosswise to the strongback. Since each station is a slightly different length at its base, you have to cut each cross cleat accordingly. (Each cleat is exactly the length of its station base.)

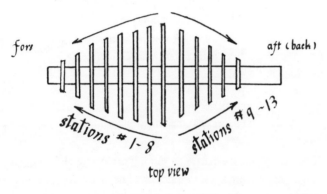

The station bevels slope in opposite direction from the middle.

Once you've measured and cut the cleats for all the stations, attach the cross cleats to the strongback. Nail the cleats squarely at the appropriate cross-line on the strongback. The cleats corresponding to stations 1-8 are nailed on the aft side of the strongback cross-lines; the cleats corresponding to stations 9-13 are nailed on the fore side of the lines.

At this point, your mold should look like a makeshift ladder.

Attach Stations to Cross Cleats

When you're in a mood to fiddle (and your patience reaches an inexhaustible level), you can line up the stations on the strongback.

Stations 1 through 8 will butt up on the fore side of the cross cleats. The remaining stations butt up against the aft side of the cleats as they march toward the transom.

With the long square in hand and two clamps nearby, set a station in place snug against its cross cleat. Now check all the references lines. The centerline you drew up the back of the station should intersect the centerline on the strongback and the baseline string above (which you strung between the plumb sticks). Make the best adjustments you can with each station, then clamp the station to its cross cleat on both sides of the strongback. Check again. When you're absolutely sure the station lines up, is on the right side of the cleat, sitting square, then screw through the station into the cross cleat.

Do this for every station.

Remember that the bevel flows from the middle station forward to the stem and from the middle station backward toward the transom.

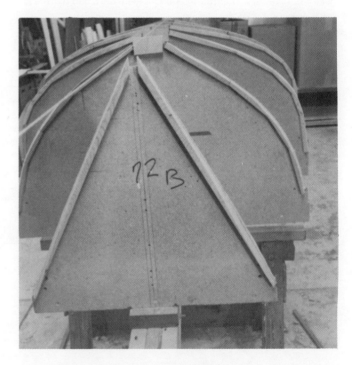

Cross cleats hold the stations to the strongback.

15

fore (stem)

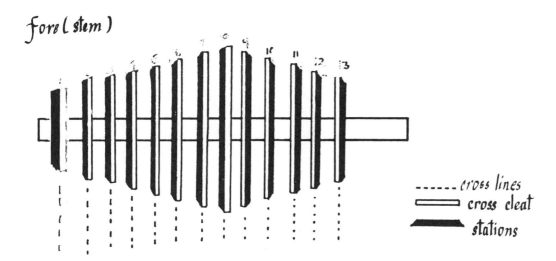

------ cross lines
▭ cross cleat
◣ stations

Cross cleats and stations assembled on the stongback.

Braces and Gussets

Your stations are up, but they need bracing. First measure the distance on the strongback between each station and cut a cleat from 2″x2″ stock. You want to run a bracing cleat station-to-station. Nail the first bracing cleat on the left side of the strongback centerline, the next bracing cleat on the right side, and so forth, alternating left and right between stations the length of the strongback.

Finally, gussy up the station-to-station bracing with gussets. Gussets are triangles you cut from ⅝″ thick particle board. Like the bracing cleats, the gussets run between stations on the strongback centerline. Each gusset butts up against the centerline you drew on the station. The upright edge of the gusset triangle should just touch the station centerline all the way up and down. Screw through the station into the gusset edge. Then screw the base of your gusset into the station-to-station bracing cleat.

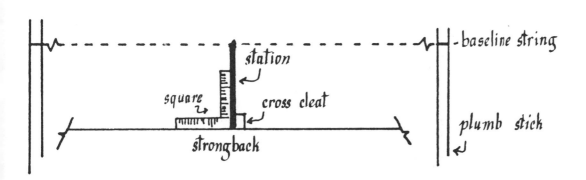

baseline string
station
square
cross cleat
strongback
plumb stick

Each station is checked for square using the large metal square laid horizontally, and then vertically, to the stongback centerline. In addition, the centerline of each station must be lined up with the baseline string.

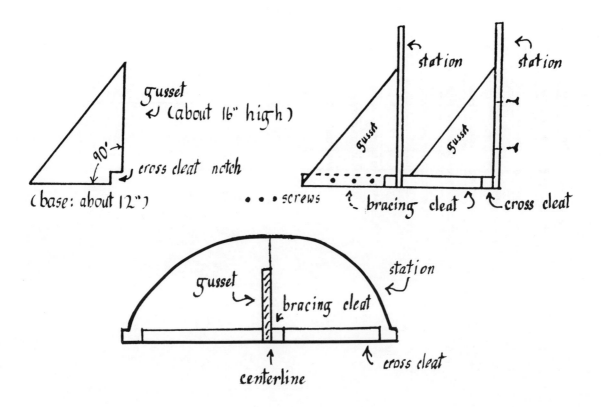

gusset
↙ (about 16" high)

90°

cross cleat notch

(base: about 12")

station

station

gusset

gusset

• • • screws

bracing cleat   cross cleat

gusset

station

bracing cleat

centerline

cross cleat

Details of gusset positioning.

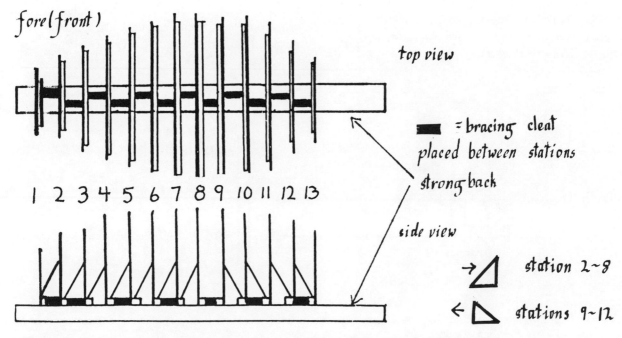

fore (front)

top view

= bracing cleat
placed between stations

strongback

1 2 3 4 5 6 7 8 9 10 11 12 13

side view

station 2~8

stations 9~12

The mold with cleats and gussets in place. Note the bracing cleats on the bottom edge of the gussets.

Transom Gusset

With your main stations reinforced on the mold, it's time to shore up the rear defenses. Measure 18 inches back of your last station and, square in hand, strike a cross-line on the strongback. This is the inside line of the transom station plate.

Cut a station-to-station bracing cleat (from 2″x2″ stock) which is 1½″ shorter than the distance from your last station to the transom plate cross-line.

Butt this bracing cleat up against your last station and nail it into place along the strongback centerline running toward the transom.

Next, study the pattern for the transom plate. Measure the base (longest line) of the transom plate and cut a cleat from 2″x2″ stock of that length. One long side of this cleat must be beveled at 15°. You can transfer that angle from the 15° angle on the transom plate pattern, or use an adjustable square. Then cut the angle into the cleat with a plane, a table saw or a skill saw. This special cleat is nailed to the strongback on the fore side of the transom plate cross-line to support the transom plate and transom.

Your last bracing task here is to cut a special gusset for the transom. This gusset is rectangular except for the side that meets the transom. That side is (you guessed it) 15°. Cut a notch so the gusset will fit over the cross cleat at the transom. Once you've cut this gusset to fit, screw it to the last station and the transom bracing cleat.

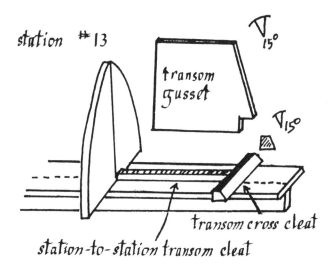

Assembly sequence for transom mold, showing 15 degree angle on transom gusset and cross cleat.

The partially assembled mold showing the transom gusset and transom plate.

After the transom has been cut out, pencil in the transom bevel line.

Using a spokeshave to bevel the transom.

Transom Plate

The transom plate is the final station on this end of the mold. Make the plate from the transom plans. (Notice that the plate is smaller than the transom on all sides and squared off at the top.)

Draw a centerline on the back of your transom plate, lean it up against the transom gusset, and line up all the lines top to bottom just as you did for the other stations. Then clamp the plate to the beveled transom cleat, check your centerlines above and below one last time, and screw the transom plate to cleat and gusset.

Transom

At long last it is time to cut the first piece that will re-main a permanent part of your rowboat—the transom. Select a ½ ″ thick piece of fine marine plywood. Exterior grade plywood is not adequate. The side you trace onto will be the outside of the transom—which will show on the finished boat—so be sure it's the best side of the plywood.

"Pin punch" through the pattern onto the plywood, tracing the outside line and the inside bevel line. Pencil in the lines, using a long strip of linoleum or flexible wood batten as a "straight edge" along the fence of small finish nails. Remember to pencil in a centerline up the transom on the outside (the beveled side).

Cut your transom on the outside line. Then, with spoke shave or small plane, bevel almost down to the inside bevel line. The final bevel cut will be made after the transom is attached to the mold.

You're ready to position and attach the transom. Lean the transom against the transom plate and position it, using the strongback centerline and the baseline string (between plumb sticks) as your reference points. (A straight piece of wood will help in the alignment).

Clamp transom to transom plate, padding the clamps so as not to mar the surface.

This end of the mold is done.

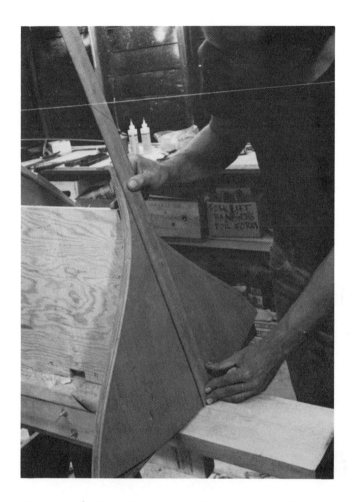

Use a straight piece of wood to help align the transom. The reference point is the baseline string.

Gluing Cleats

We now want to work forward and put in the last piece of the mold (the stem), but before we reach that point, we must install gluing cleats on all stations.

The gluing cleats, glued to the rim of the stations, will make it possible to use clamps as you assemble the hull on the mold. This means you won't have to drive nails or staples at every station where the planking passes. Your finished hull, in other words, won't be inflicted with a thousand-and-one staple or nail holes—those dark little pock marks which you often see on home boat projects.

Begin by cutting up dozens of cleats from 1"x1" stock. Each gluing cleat can be about 6" long.

Then glue a line of these cleats in a rough arc all the way around the rim of each station. Place your gluing cleats on the beveled side of the stations. Let the cleats project slightly beyond the rim of each station (they will be beveled to the right contour later.) Clamp the cleats in position until the glue dries.

Then, with a spoke shave or plane, trim the gluing cleats to conform to your bevel on each station.

You've arrived, after this long detour, at the stem, the last piece of the mold.

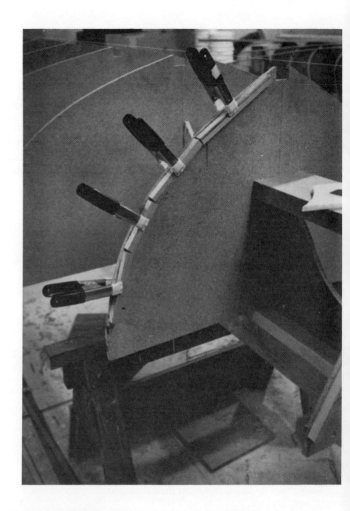

While hot-melt glue sets, gluing cleats held in place with spring clamps.

Beveling the gluing cleats with a drawknife. It is helpful to brace the mold to the floor with a temporary leg during this operation.

Stem

The stem is the second permanent piece of your boat. It remains when you discard the mold.

Place the stem pattern over a piece of ½ " marine plywood. "Pin punch" through the stem pattern, remove the pattern, and carefully cut out the stem. Notice that the stem has an inside bevel line on both sides of the stem. Bevel down to that inside line on both sides of the stem piece using a spoke shave or block plane. Lightly smooth out the stem piece with medium sandpaper.

One end of the stem fits snugly in the notch on the top of stations one and two. You can secure it there with duplex (double-headed) nails for easy removal later.

The other end of the stem sits on the strongback. To keep it in place there, measure and cut a "square horseshoe" from ¾ " plywood or particle board. This trap piece is placed around the stem end on the strongback. Be sure to center the "square horseshoe" on the strongback centerline. You don't want your stem out of whack.

The stem end takes quite a bit of force as the planks bend and taper dramatically here. Notice that we installed a 2 "x6 " brace between stations #1 and #2 as a fresh reinforcement. The horseshoe we simply clamped to the strongback, but you can glue or nail it in, too.

Stem horseshoe clamped on the strongback. Note: Station #1 is not shown.

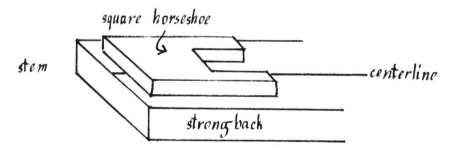

Positioning of the horseshoe on the strongback.

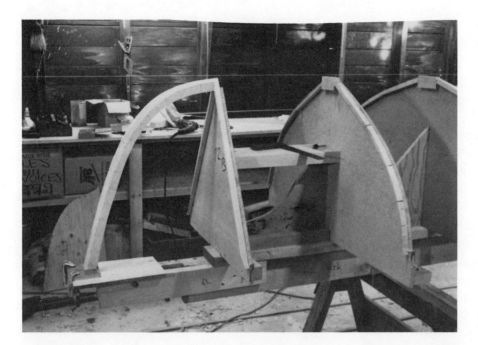

Fairing

Your mold is up. Now all it needs is a little refinement.

Before you begin the actual building of this great boat, you need to fair the mold. Fairing now will insure clear sailing ahead (and hide a multitude of sins later).

Fairing refers first to "eyeballing" your mold from every possible angle. Do the bevels flow neatly fore and aft on your mold? If not, shave here and sand there. Try to get everything just so. Sculpt this turkey so you can dress it right.

Fairing is an art, but you can be artful without being experienced in boatbuilding. Select one of the cedar strips you intend to build your boat hull with, grab three or four spring clamps, and do some test runs. Clamp this strip into actual position along the stations. Now eyeball the plank. Is it bulging at a station where it should be running smooth? Sand and shave that station. Try the plank there again. Try the test plank in other positions. Be sure it hugs your mold snug and true.

Then, when you're satisfied that everything is as close to ideal as you want to make it ("fair enough" if not "absolutely perfect"), reach for a roll of strapping tape.

Tape over all the outside edges of each station. Where the planks touch the stations, glue can seep through. And there's really only one disastrous error you can make when you build this boat: that's to glue the hull to the mold. So tape the station edges. Where plank touches mold, you do not want a lasting bond. This is a superior rowboat, but even it will not row well with its mold aboard.

A plank clamped in place to begin the fairing process.

Planking The Hull

Building the hull of your boat is more satisfying than the fidgety business of mold assembly. You can finally clothe that bare wooden skeleton with a flashy cedar-strip planking.

The Cosine Wherry rowboat is constructed of narrow ¼"x¾"—16' long red cedar strips. You start at the bottom and work up (sounds like real life), strip by strip, clamping each strip to the mold stations, gluing one strip to the next. You stop at the waterline and then work down from the keel line plank by plank. (Later, you seal and fiberglass the hull, throw out the mold, turn the boat right side up, and finish the inside.)

The advantage of our glue-and-clamp approach will be evident to every eye. You end up with a smooth, unmarred hull—no telltale speckles where staples or nails might have been used to secure planks to stations during construction. The hull comes off unpocked. The clamps which hold the planks in place on the mold while the glue dries leave no unsightly blemishes.

Planking in this way is foolproof. If you make a mistake in positioning a cedar strip, you can back up and get it right. Patience is, once again, the only virtue you need. The skills are undoubtedly ones you already possess. And the only "unusual" tools you need are a hot-melt glue gun and some spring clamps.

Materials for Planking

¼"x¾" (VG) red cedar strips, 16' lengths (straight, dry)
3 gal. epoxy resin solution (2 gallons resin plus 1 gallon hardener)

Tools for Planking

Spring clamps (8 is the minimum number, up to 19 is best)
Hot-melt glue gun (with wood glue cartridges)
1" push pins or nail pads
Finish nails
Pencil
Utility knife
Long board hand sander
Orbital sander
Triangular scraper or 2" cabinet scraper
Small block plane
Wide "paint" container
Squeegee, brushes, disposable gloves, respirator
Bar clamp (optional)

Keel Strip

Run your first red cedar strip over the top center of the stations from keel to stem. Let one end of the strip hang out over the transom. (You can saw it off at the transom later.) Clamp the strip in position. Eyeball it for

Keel strip in place; view of aft stations.

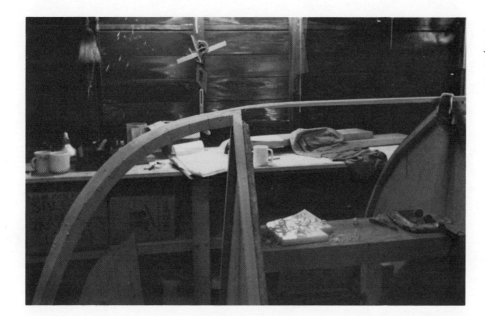

Keel strip in place; view of forward stations. This strip helps to keep the stations straight and the stem in place.

straightness, curve, and centering. The baseline string will help you fair it up. When you're satisfied with the shape and alignment of the keel strip, use small finishing nails to secure the strip to the transom and each of the stations.

At the stem, use your draw knife, plane, or utility knife to cut a gradual taper in the strip so that it flows fairly smoothly into the stem. Nail the tapered end of the plank to the stem with a finishing nail.

The nails do not have to go all the way in. You'll want to remove them later.

You can remove one item: the baseline string between plumb sticks. It's no longer needed.

Plank Along Sheerline

Load up your hot-melt glue gun and practice on a few scraps of wood before you take a real shot at gluing the planks of your hull. As Lee, our boatbuilder, discovered, hot-melt is "hot with a capital OUCH," so be careful.

Once you see how your glue gun acts, you're ready to lay your first planks.

The first 3 cedar strips you lay on each side of the mold are crucial. They determine how the rest of the planking will go (smooth, straight, orderly of course), so take your time.

Start on one side of the mold, pick up a cedar strip, and center it at the middle station. Let it rest in the station notch at the sheerline (the bottom line of the mold.) Clamp it in place at the middle station and then work it around the stations, working a little ways fore and then a little ways aft, clamping it here and there to a station. (Clamp from underneath the strip. You'll soon be placing a second strip on top of the first one and you don't want clamps in the way.)

Now eyeball your first strip carefully. You may want to do some last moment fairing of the mold.

When your first strip seems straight and snug, nail (with finish nail) or staple it to the transom, stem, and each station.

Warm your glue gun. Ready a second cedar strip. You'll again be working from the middle, first a foot or so fore, then a foot or so aft. Be sure you have your second cedar strip in the right position so that it will meet the stem and hang over the transom. (Where the planks hang over the transom you will eventually saw off the excess.) Take a deep breath, relax, and put down a modest, but unbroken bead of glue along the top of your first plank. Run it along a few inches.

The first strips glued into place. Note: The clamps holding the stem should not be necessary with molds using a #1 station. In this case, #1 station was not used.

Now place your second cedar strip in position and push it down against the first plank. Hold it tight with your fingers for a full minute so the glue can catch and cool. You've got it! Now all you have to do is keep gluing along the strip, pinching, and waiting—a few feet forward and a few feet back of the middle station—until that strip is glued on. To hold the glued strip in position on the stations, use a second set of clamps (at each station if you have enough clamps). As you reach the stem and transom, nail (or staple) the second strip down at the two end points only. Leave all the clamps on for awhile. Let the glue really set up. You should be pinching the planks together as hard as you can. Glue should ooze out between the planks here and there. (Don't worry, you can easily remove excess glue later.)

You may meet resistance as you bend a strip around certain stations. Don't be intimidated. Your aim is to force the inside edges of joined planks hard together. You can feel this inside joint with your fingers as you press. Don't worry about the tiny gaps between planks on the outside surface; just be sure the inner point of the seam is tight.

There are now two planks on, glued together all the way along, nailed at both ends, held to the stations above and below by spring clamps. STOP. It is crucial that you equalize the stripping process, so go to the other side of the hull and secure the first two strips there. Perhaps the best way to maintain equilibrium is to go one strip at a time around the whole boat, alternating from side to side.

Your next step, then, is to glue and clamp a third cedar strip in place on both sides of the mold. You have to remove clamps as you go, of course, moving them up to hold your third plank as you glue it onto the second plank.

You've now installed 6 planks, three on each side. They define the graceful sheer of your hull.

Nail Pads, Push Pins, Clamps

You can now keep adding strips, two at a time, first on one side of the mold, then on the other, up to the waterline of the hull. But let's pause for some inside tips on planking.

The higher you travel up the mold, the more likely you are to encounter stress and torque as you try to bend your planks into position. You may have to resort to minor acts of violence—or at least of strength—to get a bend here and there. In fact, the spring clamps alone may not always be enough to hold a portion of the strip in correct position as it dries. A glued plank may bulge out or even jump free of a station when you turn your back on it.

Fortunately, you have no reason to curse, wail, or strike back with a sledge hammer when a plank refuses to stay put. There are ways out of such disasters.

The cleverest solution is the nail pad. A nail pad is simply a small block of ⅛″ or ¼″ plywood with a 1″ (box or common) nail driven through it. The wood block is taped so it won't stick to the glue. To hold a stubborn plank snug to its station, you can nail a pad *between* strips at any station point. The pad will hold the planks firmly in—and the nail in the nail pad passes into the station without marring the planks. (Nail pads are so effective, you could practically build this boat without spring clamps, using only nail pads. But we recommend you use nail pads only where spring clamps aren't doing the job.)

A similar device is the push pin. Again, you can insert a push pin *between* planks, the wide head of the push pin acting as a pad on the two planks.

We used push pins between planks quite often when we built this rowboat, but we found that nail pads did the same job and were stronger. We could not find push pins that were long enough (shaft at least 1″) and stout enough to hold well.

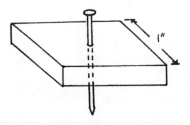

Nail pad used to hold planks in position against the stations. The nail is inserted between the planks.

A few times, we resorted to using wood battens, held at each end by a clamp, to secure sections of planking that wanted to pull away from a station. Station #1 at the stem, where the planking bend is severe, proved the most stubborn. In fact, the stem itself tends to pull out of alignment as you put on the first few planks. To hold the stem in line, we used a bar clamp between stem and station #2. After we had a number of planks glued in, we took the bar clamp off.

Our philosophy of bracing is that anything that works without marring the planks is worth using.

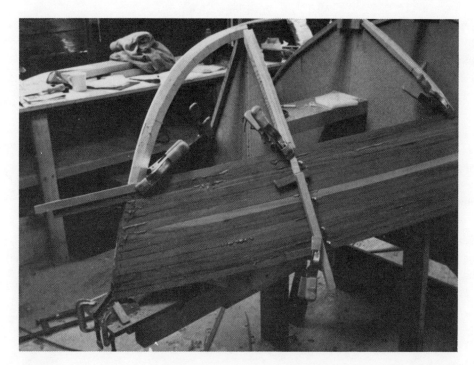

A wooden holding strip is clamped in place to hold the boat strips tight against the mold. A nail pad could also be used here.

Plank to Waterline

After you glue and clamp the first three cedar strips on each side of the mold, you simply keep building the hull strip by strip.

You no longer need a solid bead of glue. A dab every 6″ is plenty.

Don't get ahead on one side of the mold. Unless you attend equally to both sides of the mold, the hull will try to twist itself apart. Alternate sides, adding one strip at a time.

Place exactly *19* strips on each side of the hull and *STOP*. You're about at the waterline. It is now time to lock in these planks.

Strip Tips

You're half-finished planking your boat. While you pause, here are some construction tips:

- Work out a way to set the glue gun aside quickly as you work. If you drop it, you may have to buy another one. We ruined our first gun that way. They do break.

- Apply a thin bead of glue to planks. It will be plenty.

- It's all but impossible to work with more than a foot of glued planking at a time.

- As you glue, hold the plank in place at least 30 seconds. A full minute might be better.

- Squeeze the inside edge of planks together as the glue cools. Make the inside of the hull as smooth and tight as possible.

- Strips in twisty areas must be held down a long time before the glue really grabs. That's why clamps, nail pads, and push pins can be a godsend.

- A misaligned strip can be repositioned. Free it up with a knife by cutting into the glue; then pry it gently into correct position after you shoot in fresh hot glue. Press the errant plank into its new position and hold for a minute.

- How the strips line up on the inside is more important than how they line up on the outside of the hull. Get the strips tight and straight on the inside.

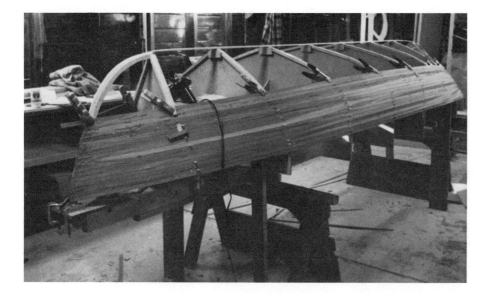

The hull planked as far as the transition point. This is where the planking pattern changes. From this point on you will plank from the keel down. Note the use of nail pads and push pins.

Removing excess glue.

Remove Excess Glue

Once the planks from sheer to waterline have been glued and set up for several days, take your chisel or scraper and gently remove the runs and globs of glue from the hull. Scrape slowly and avoid gouging the cedar strips.

Epoxy

To glue the first 19 planks securely to each other, apply a mixture of epoxy resin and hardener to which wood flour has been added. Be sure that whatever you use is an epoxy resin; nothing grips cedar so well.

Mix up 6 ounces of epoxy (2 parts A to 1 part B). Mix thoroughly. A wide, low container keeps the resin from hardening too fast—a cake pan or disposable pie pan will do. The secret to a proper epoxy mixture at this stage is adding enough phenolic microballoons (or wood flour). Microballoons are simply opaque thickeners for the glue resin. The hot-melt glue dries clear, but the epoxy you now add will be opaque (meaning you won't see sunlight between the planks when the hull is completely dry). Aim for a consistency similar to that of thick cream.

The partially planked hull after applying epoxy.

Apply the epoxy directly. You can use a brush, a roller—you can even pour it on—and a rubber squeegee is the ideal instrument to force the epoxy into gaps. In fact, that's your purpose here—get the epoxy between the planks. Leave as little excess epoxy on the surface of each plank as possible. Whatever is left on the outside of the hull must be sanded off later.

While you apply the filler, disposable gloves and a respirator (face mask to block fumes) are musts.

Let the epoxy harden at least 24 hours (if the room temperature remains at 70°F—48 hours if the temperature is around 50°F).

Plank Down From Keel to Transition Line

Begin at the keel strip on top of the mold and finish the planking of the hull. Your first 3 or 4 strips on both sides of the keel line take extreme bends, so you might begin by nailing them lightly to the transom.

Work from the middle station as before, gluing fore a bit, then aft.

At the stem, you will have to get out your trusty utility knife and carve a rough, tapered angle so that the first hull strip meets the keel strip evenly. The blade cuts through red cedar as it would through cold butter. (The trim and taper don't have to be exact because you'll sand the point where planks meet stem later.)

Use your clamps, nail pads, or push-pins generously.

At a point five or six planks down from the keel, you'll probably find that your next plank just won't bend into position. We ran into that. We kept trying to put the plank into position and hold it there. It simply wouldn't hold. You could almost hear it lifting off. So at that point we used a stealer. A stealer is simply part of a plank about two feet long. We trimmed one end of our short plank to fit the stem, nailed it with a finish nail to the stem, drew a diagonal line from the lower stem edge, then tapering back to the upper end of the stealer, and cut along this line with our knife. We glued it to the plank above it and clamped it in. The stealer, in other words, is a short "cheater plank." Once you insert a cheater on the stem, you find that the rest of your cedar strips fit more easily.

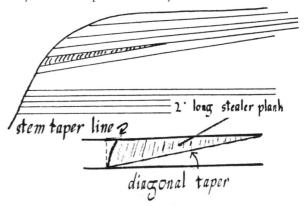

Stealer, cut from a plank about two feet long.

The planking pattern from the keel to the transition point. The stealer is fitted to prevent having a reverse bend in the plank below it.

Taper Planks at Transition Point

On the eleventh strip down from the keel, our upper plank met head-on with the 19 lower planks we started days earlier. Since our upper planks intersect the lower ones at an arc, we must trim the ends of the strips to join the lower ones securely and gracefully.

These intersection tapers look difficult, but they are rather easy to cut and shape.

First, allow the plank to hang over the transition line. With a pencil, mark the point on one edge of the plank where it intersects the lower planks—and mark a point on the other side of the overlapping plank surface where it again intersects the lower plank. Connect your two marks with a straight line. Then cut along that line with a sharp knife. See if the tapered plank fits. You may have to use a plane to take a little more off the taper. If you're patient, tapered joints are fun to cut, shape, and glue. Don't make the tapered joint super-tight; you want glue to penetrate between all planks. Nail pads or push pins will help hold things together at this great intersection in the hull.

Continue planking down, cutting tapers on both ends to fit snug at the transition point. When you slip in the last glued plank, you are through planking this boat forever.

Scribing a plank.

Cutting the plank with a utility knife.

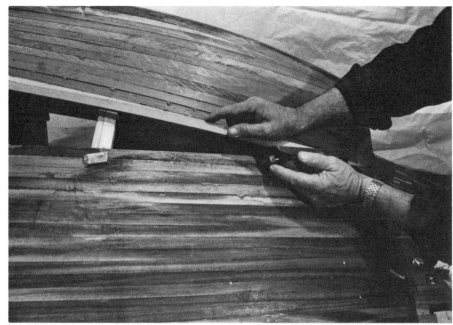

Dressing the taper with a block plane for the final fit.

The fitted planks.

The planking is near completion.

Epoxy Glue

Scrape off excess glue and apply epoxy resin following the same procedure described earlier. Admire the completed hull—and by the way, congratulations: *it does look like a boat at last!*

The hull completely planked and epoxied.

Sand Smooth

To ready the outside of the hull for the final step (fiberglassing), you must smooth and fair it from stem to stern and from sheer to keel.

First, saw off those over-reaching ends of the planks at the transom.

Second, remove the excess resin from the surface area of the planks. Apply paint remover, let it sit for 15 minutes, then eliminate the resin from the planks with your scraper.

Third, begin a complete finish sanding.

Red cedar scratches easily, so we recommend hand sanding. A long board works extremely well, and you can build one quickly. The base of the long board is ⅛" plywood; the two handles on either end, screwed in from below, can be fashioned in any shape from whatever materials strike your fancy. The sandpaper is then tacked on with disc adhesive—or you can buy adhesive sandpaper.

Start sanding the entire hull with 50 grit sandpaper. Knock off all corners, rounding them gracefully (especially on the stem). Sand diagonally to the plank lines. This is the way to remove small irregularities without gouging into the wood. Sand until you eliminate all scraper marks.

For your next sanding, use your orbital sander with medium (80 grit) sandpaper. Lastly, switch to 120 grit sandpaper for a superb, smooth finish.

If you are a perfectionist, lightly mop the hull with water; this will highlight scratches and tell you where to keep sanding.

And if you are a realist, you might agree with our own boat-builder's strip tip #99:

"To hell with perfect fits—it's only a boat!"

Fairing the hull with a longboard.

If you've never fiberglassed, you might think it's a formidable, highly technical task. It's not.

On the other hand, if you have applied fiberglass before, you're not likely to rate it ahead of a vacation cruising the Caribbean.

Fiberglassing is actually a simple task, as straightforward as painting a picket fence. In fact, if you can paint a fence, you're fully qualified to fiberglass the hull of your rowboat. It may not be a pleasure, but neither is it a punishment. And the results are spectacular.

Fiberglass helps hold the boat together, lowers your yearly maintenance, protects the red cedar planks, and preserves the beauty of wood (which is a special feature of this boat).

Materials for Fiberglassing the Hull

4" fiberglass tape, 4 or 6 oz., 60'
5 sheets of 6 oz. fiberglass cloth, 5'wide by 15' long
Epoxy resin mixture, 2 gallons
¾" x ¾" spruce, 12' (keel)
¾" x 6" spruce, 2' (skeg)
Phenolic microballoons (or wood flour)

Tools for Fiberglassing

Scissors
Paint brushes
Squeegee
"Paint" containers (wide and low)
Measuring cup
Disposable gloves
Barrier cream
Hand sander (Long board)
Disk Sander (low speed, soft pad)
Respirator (a sophisticated version of a dust mask)
Jig saw
Block plane
Wood rasp, rough half-oval, about 14"

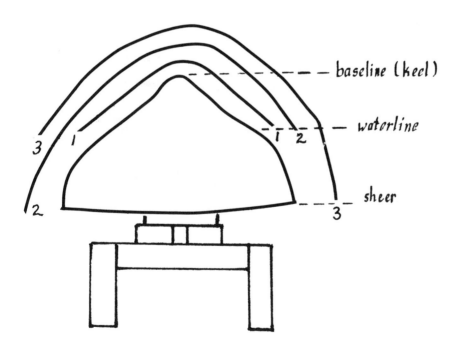

Layering of fiberglass cloth on the outside of the hull. If your objective is to keep the boat as lightweight as possible, layer #1 can be eliminated.

Lay Out the Fiberglass Cloth

The fiberglass cloth we recommend is 60" wide, 15' long. Your first task is to lay it over the hull on the keel (the baseline) so that 30" hangs down on each side of the hull. Handle the cloth somewhat gingerly; you don't want to pull it out of shape any more than necessary. Pretend you are setting the table for 2,000 world-renowned boatbuilders.

The hull itself should first be dusted and vacuumed. Any crumb left under this table cloth will be pinned to the hull for good.

Your first sheet hangs over the waterline on both sides of the hull. You want it to hang over the waterline just a couple inches. Grab your oldest, strongest scissors and trim the cloth on both sides so it hangs just below the transition point. (The transition point is the line on the hull where the first 19 planks intersect with the planks you laid down from the keel.) Carefully rescue and fold the waste you trim off as you cut the cloth around the hull. You'll use these scraps later.

Both the stem and the bottom edges of the transom need to be slightly rounded so the cloth will lay flat at these points. Do that rounding now with a rasp. At the stem, cut out a triangular section from the overhanging cloth so that you can press the cloth snugly to the stem with only a minimum overlap. Ideally, you want a 1" overlap of cloth on the stem piece.

At the transom, you want only about an inch to overlap the edges of the transom. Trim here if necessary.

As you work the cloth, we assume you're wearing gloves and a mask—fiberglass fibers are prickly, irritating, and make bad neighbors in your lungs.

The bottom outside of the hull will be protected by three overlapping layers of fiberglass cloth. Since you must apply epoxy to each layer separately, your next step is to use epoxy on the cloth you now have in position over the keel.

The overall layout system for fiberglass you are using provides three tough layers below the water, one strong layer on each side above the water. That's more than enough protection for all the seasons to come. Your second layer will begin on one side at the sheer, drape over the keel, and run down the other side of the hull to the waterline. You'll have to trim it to fit. The third sheet of fiberglass cloth goes in the opposite direction, running from the sheer on the other side of the hull, over the keel, down to the waterline.

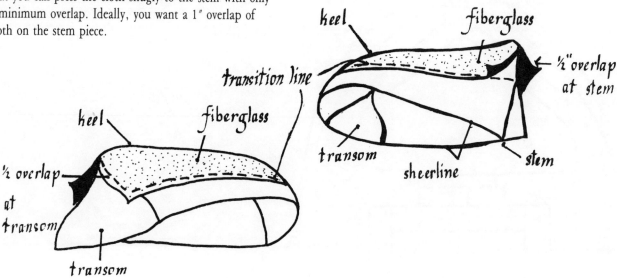

Fiberglass cloth overlaps fore and aft, doubling the strength at points of stress.

Cutting the gore, or triangular section, at the stem.

A caution: WORK CLEAN. Fiberglass and the epoxy you spread over it have no business entering the human body. Following unprotected exposure to glass and chemicals, some workers experience allergic reactions. It may take weeks, even months, before a reaction appears, so by all means protect yourself. Remove watch, rings, and other attachments. You might want to rub some "barrier cream" into your skin. Disposable gloves are indispensable aids in applying epoxies safely. So is the wearing of the respirator dust mask. Ventilation in the workshop area is a plus.

Epoxy the Fiberglass

Your task is not only to coat the fiberglass cloth with epoxy resin, but to do so quickly and without creating major creases, pulls, and unsightly wrinkles in the cloth. We've found that a squeegee is the best tool to meet these goals.

Make up a batch of epoxy—no more than a quart—and mix it throughly in a paper cup or measuring container. Pour your mix into a wide, shallow container. (Epoxy hardens quickly when exposed to air and when exposed to itself in mixed form. It will last you longer if you spread it out on a wide palate before you coat your masterpiece.)

Those of you who are well-versed in Zen will do splendidly at this point; the rest of us will simply muddle through, working as quickly and carefully as we can.

You can apply epoxy with any tool that suits your fancy. Some use a brush, some use a roller, and some literally pour it on. But no matter how you apply it, work from top center out and down in all directions. In other words, start at the central area of the keel, spreading the epoxy out and down, fanning out like the spokes of a wheel. (Don't fight gravity; you'll lose.) Working from the center out and down also keeps the cloth flat.

As the epoxy resin runs, the squeegee can catch it. Wipe the resin as thin as possible — but leave no fiber of the cloth unpenetrated. Go with the weave of the cloth. If you pull diagonally to the weave, you can close up the fibers, preventing the epoxy from fully penetrating those inner chambers of strength.

As you spread the epoxy, you will probably see some cloth folds develop. This happens to everyone (except a few Michelangelos of Fiberglassing). Since your boat is not the Sistine Chapel, don't panic when folds appear. Try to work them out, pulling ever so gently as you spread the resin with your squeegee. The squeegee is often effective in persuading the cloth to right itself.

Applying the epoxy resin with a squeegee. Note how the cloth becomes transparent when saturated.

Leave no unclothed, uncoated gaps. You may end up with a wrinkle or pull here and there, but don't despair. These will be invisible by the time you're done with the hull. Air bubbles that may appear under the glass can be stippled out with a short bristled brush.

Allow the first layer of cloth to cure for at least 48 hours—longer if you can hold yourself back. Heat lamps can speed up the process, but patience is the best cure. If you try to sand resin before it is cured, you'll create a buttery smear quite difficult to remove. So be patient, please.

After curing, sand the hull with coarse (40 grit) sandpaper to knock down wrinkles and loose ends. Fold your sandpaper over a ''hard block'' (a 2″ x 4″ x 6″ block of wood) and handle it like a file. This is a brush-back sanding designed to eliminate high spots.

You're now ready to fiberglass your second layer of cloth.

Position, Epoxy, and Sand Twice More

Position a second sheet of fiberglass cloth (running from sheer over keel to the transition point and trim to fit. Apply epoxy as before, let it cure a few days, then do a "brushback" sanding.

Finally, repeat the fiberglassing with a third run of cloth.

You now have 3 overlapping layers of cloth below and one layer on each side above the transition point.

Fiberglass the Transom

Retrieve one of your fiberglass cloth scraps and cut it to fit the transom. Trim it so that it just hangs over the edge of the transom onto the planking. A half inch is ideal.

Mix up a small batch of epoxy and apply it to the fiberglass you've laid on the transom. (Work top to bottom—keel to sheer—with the weave.)

Don't put away the epoxy yet.

Epoxy and Sand Hull Again

Coat the entire hull with epoxy, just as you did before.

Wait at least 48 hours. Sand with medium sandpaper again. Sand hull and transom. You can sand with a little more vigor now.

Epoxy and Sand One More Time

Ever feel like you've been caught in a revolving door? Too bad. Apply a third coat of resin, let cure a few days, then sand the hull and transom once again.

Skeg and Keel

Before you release the hull from the mold and attack the interior, you must put the finishing touches to the bottom of your boat.

The skeg is a triangular piece of spruce lumber which attaches to the bottom under the transom; the keel piece is a long strip of spruce which flows from the skeg forward to the stem along the keel line.

The purpose of the skeg and keel is to provide a rugged base for the boat—a buffer between the hull and whatever the boat scrapes against (be it dry land, a rocky shore, or a parking lot) when in use, transport, or storage. The keel is actually a sacrificial piece into which you will later fasten a brass or bronze plate (the rub shoe) without penetrating (and possibly weakening) the fiberglassed hull. You are in effect building a landing strip which will add strength and beauty to this vessel. The skeg helps the boat track straight as it moves through the water.

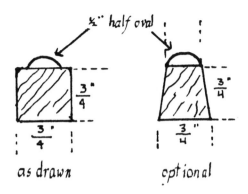

Cross section of two different possibilities for the keel.

Cut Out Skeg and Keel

Fish through the boat plans for the skeg pattern. The skeg is made from ¾ " spruce lumber, so locate a suitable piece.

Transfer the outline of the skeg by tracing from the plans through a sheet of carbon paper onto a sheet of newspaper or wrapping paper. The carbon paper will leave the lines of the skeg on the paper under it. With scissors, cut that paper pattern, place it on your spruce lumber, and pencil its outline on the wood. Then saw out your skeg.

The keel piece is fashioned from ¾ " thick, ¾ " wide, 12-foot long spruce. It may be beveled at about 15° on both long sides so that a ½ " wide brass or bronze half oval rub shoe can be attached later.

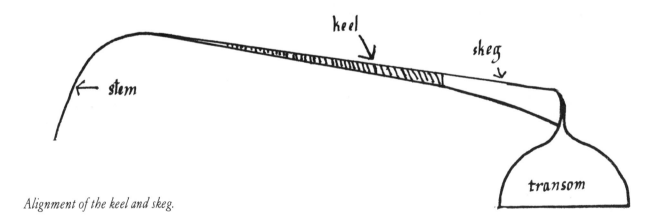

Alignment of the keel and skeg.

Install Skeg and Keel

Sand back a narrow corridor along the keel line of the hull where the skeg and keel piece will be placed (don't sand to bare wood, just rough up the epoxy). This corridor need not be precise since you will soon glass these pieces into the hull.

Skeg and keel are initially held in place by thickened epoxy. Try out the pieces for fit, then thicken up epoxy with phenolic microballoons (or wood flour) to the consistency of heavy cream, then glue them on.

We held these glued pieces in place with sandbags (any heavy item will do), placing sheets of plastic between sandbags and wood. The last thing you want to do is glue sandbags to the bottom of your boat!

The skeg glued in place.

The keel being glued on. Note the sandbags and the poke extending down from the ceiling.

Fair and Fillet

When the glue has hardened, gently round off the areas where the hull meets the keel and skeg with the rasp. Fair this joint so you have a ¼″ radius "cove."

Then, to insure a strong fiberglassing, sculpture a fillet along both sides of these keel pieces. A fillet is simply a length of putty which creates a smooth, curved transition between the hull and the keel and skeg. (Since fiberglass has trouble turning sharp corners, it relies on a fillet to cushion abrupt joints such as the one you've just built.)

The fillet is a thick putty of resin to which you add phenolic microballoons. (For microballons, you can substitute milled fiber, chopped linen, or sanding dust.) First mix your resin and hardener, then add the microballoons. Make the mixture thicker than you really think anyone ever has before—300 cc as stiff as peanut butter is about right for a fillet. Apply your fillet (sometimes called coving putty) all the way along the keel piece and skeg on both sides in a gentle curve. We used a beer can (about 2″ in diameter) to form the fillet near the transom, and then a 1″ diameter can to form the fillet forward of the skeg.

Let your fillet harden a day or two, then rasp it fair to the hull.

Fiberglass

To glass in the keel piece, use three 4″ wide lengths of fiberglass tape (4 oz. or 6 oz.). Drape the first piece of tape over the length of the keel and apply resin. Do the same for the next two tape strips, allowing time to dry between each layer. Offset and overlap the three tape strips slightly for added strength—and sand with coarse sandpaper (40 or 50 grit) between each layer. It's the waiting around between layers, of course, that takes time.

The skeg is glassed in the same way as the keel piece, except that you'll need to use a scrap of fiberglass cloth as a final layer (trimmed and draped over the skeg so that it overlaps fillets and an inch or two of the hull planking). Again, sand between cloth layers.

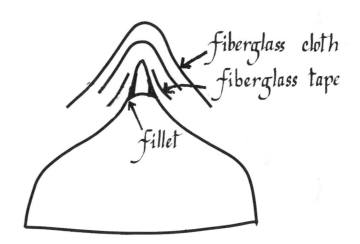

Suggested glassing sequence for the skeg and keel.

Fairing the fillet along the skeg.

Glassing the skeg using scrap cloth. Along the keel, 4 inch tape works best.

Final Fairing

Grab your old friend—the Long Board—and fair up the entire hull with 50-grit sandpaper. This is your last chance to smooth the shell of your boat (unless you want to keep glassing and sanding . . . a routine that can be addictive in rare cases).

Sand, sand, sand away, until it seems you're almost down to the cloth. You should see no glassy spots on the hull; as veteran boatbuilders say, everything is "standing smooth." Any irregularity you can feel with your fingertips will show later to the eye, so be particular about your fairing.

When the smoothness satisfies you, power sand the entire hull with 80-grit sandpaper—and apply a final coat of epoxy resin.

Let this final coat harden, admire the glistening hull, and relax. The hardest work is over. You have built a laminated boat shell of cedar strips and fiberglass—a hull which requires no other structural support . . . the hull of a light, strong, finely crafted wooden boat.

The hull is now ready to be removed from the mold.

You can now focus on finishing the interior of your rowboat. It needs to be smoothed out and fiberglassed, but it won't need as many coats as the exterior did. (After all, this boat is water tight.)

Since you're experienced now with sanding and fiberglassing, this phase should go like clockwork. (Nothing ever goes like clockwork, of course, especially in the time-honored tradition of fine small boatbuilding, but why not approach it with zealous confidence?)

Materials & Tools

You'll need most of the things you've already used, including those scraps of fiberglass cloth you saved and carefully laid aside.

Flip the Hull

Time to free the mold from the hull. If you taped your stations, there shouldn't be much glue standing between you and an upright, mold-free boat hull.

With you on one end and a friend on the other, see if the hull is willing to budge. Stoop down and press from the inside out on the hull to free it from stubborn points of resistance.

Once you start making headway, the mold should stay down and the hull should ascend, free of its skeleton.

Set your boat gingerly aside and carry the mold to some dark and dusty corner. (Save the mold. It was real work to put it together, and you never know when someone else—or even you yourself—will want to build another Cosine Wherry.)

Place your hull (upright, of course) on new support.

The mold can now be removed from the sawhorses. Use the sawhorses to make a cradle to hold the boat. Simply nail two padded boards (2x4's will do fine) across the sawhorses. These boards need to be long enough and spaced far enough apart to hold the boat whether upside down or right side up.

Scrape, Fill, and Sand

The interior of your boat is replete with glue drippings and rough edges, so your first task is to scrape away excess epoxy. This will take several hours—and you'll discover that it was easier to remove such excesses on the outside. (Inside the hull, the curve works against a careful scraping.)

Keep your scraper sharp and file it often (rounding the outside edges of the blade so it won't catch or dig into the interior wood). Work your scraper diagonally in both directions, then fore and aft in line with the planks. Shavings should peel off neatly.

Scrape until the interior is relatively smooth and even, but don't aim for a "violin finish." We do want to get this boat done and in the water sometime—right?

The hull, scraped and with the corners at the transom filleted. Note the fillet extends along the keel line.

Fillets in place at the stem. This fillet also extends a short distance down the keel line.

Next, form fillets where the transom and the stem meet the interior planks. Mix a stiff (very stiff) putty out of the epoxy and microballons (or other filling) just as you did for the fillets along the external keel. Cove the putty along the seams or joints of the transom and also at the stem so that you create a gracefully rounded transition which your fiberglass can follow. Let the putty cure, then sand the fillet with 50-grit paper until reasonably fair.

Finally, with 4″ fiberglass tape, glass the area you have just filleted. Apply three layers of tape. Epoxy each taped layer separately, let it dry, and sand between coats.

Now fair up the whole interior with 80-grit sandpaper on your orbital or disc sander.

Cloth Layout

Glassing the interior won't take many hours, but since each layer must be fitted and epoxied separately you will have to spread out this preparation over a few days as you wait for the resin to cure.

The overall layout is simple. The first two panels of fiberglass cloth cover the bottom of the boat up the sides to the waterline on each side (the waterline is about where the upper 19 planks meet the lower planks). The other two panels run up from the waterline to the sheer (the top plank or edge of the boat), one panel on each side.

This means you will cover the bottom with two center panels and the sides above the waterline with one panel each.

Just two 60″ wide, 14-foot long runs of cloth will do the whole job.

Fit and Trim First Panel

Lay the first panel in the bottom of the boat lengthwise. Let one side of the cloth drape over the edge so it hangs outside the boat. Tape the other side of the panel to the interior side of the hull so that it is above the waterline all the way along. Use small strips of masking tape every foot or so to hold the cloth up on the side.

Now for the trimming. First, trim the panel of fiberglass at the stern so it overlaps the transom by ½ ″. Cut a straight slot in the glass at the bottom of the transom (where it meets the keel line) a foot or so forward along the bottom of the boat. This slot enables you to pull the cloth slightly so it overlaps as it touches the bottom directly in front of the transom.

Trim the panel at the stem, too, slotting it so it overlaps.

Finally, trim the sides of the cloth (both sides). As your trimming guide, select and follow the seam of a plank on each side that is about 2½ ″ above the planking transition. Use pieces of tape as you trim along the sides to keep the panel from tumbling down.

You should end up with a trim panel which covers the inside from transition to transition fore and aft.

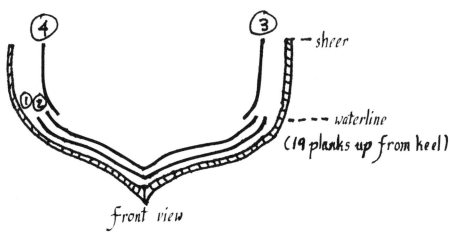

Using 60 inch fiberglass cloth, this is the suggested glassing sequence for the inside of the hull.

Fitting glass aft.

Fitting glass forward.

Triming the glass along the tansition point.

Glass cloth fitted and ready for resin. Notice the masking tape that keeps the cloth in place while you apply the epoxy.

Glass and Peel the Center Panel

Wet the center panel with epoxy, spreading it evenly with a rubber squeegee.

As this resin jells—but before it fully hardens—take your reliable utility knife and carefully slice away about 1″ of resined panel on each side, peeling away the tape and resin as you go. As a trimming guide, select a hull plank and follow its seam. Allow to cure, then sand and fair the edges so it is smooth.

Remember, you want no hard ridges where panels meet and overlap, so always feather raw edges with sandpaper before fiberglassing another panel.

Complete the Second Center Panel

Fit and trim a second panel directly over the first central layer. Do it exactly as you did the first panel. Trim and tape it a few inches above the transition point on both sides, apply resin, and then cut and peel away the tape and resin excess above the transition.

Boatbuilding is nothing if not repetitious at times.

Two layers of glass completed on the bottom. The boat is now ready for the side layers of cloth.

Peeling away the one inch strip of glass and unhardened resin from the center panel.

Fit, Trim, and Glass the Two Side Panels

The two side panels are left over from the two center panels. Let the cut edge hang over the sheer out of the boat. Position the uncut edge of each panel so it drops just below the transition point, overlapping the double-strength bottom fiberglassing. Spring clamps will hold the side panels in position. Clothes pins work, too.

Now wet the side panels with epoxy and spread carefully with the trusty squeegee. Remove clamps as you work along.

After the cure is complete, trim off the excess cloth along the sheer. Allow the sides to cure for a few days.

Fitting the side panel.

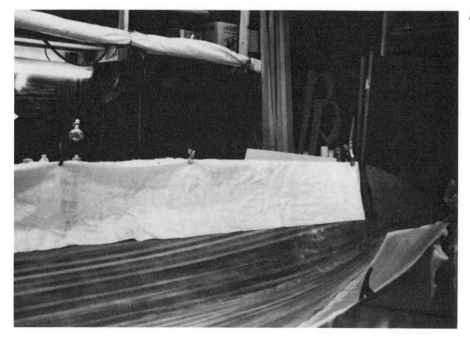

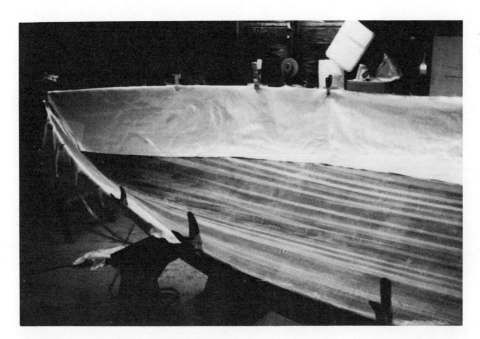

Both side panels fitted and ready to epoxy.

Glass the Transom

Trim a scrap of fiberglass cloth to fit the inside face of the transom. The cloth should lap over the fillets.

Pour and spread the epoxy.

Sand, Feather, and Epoxy

One more big step:

Lightly sand back the whole interior by hand with 40-grit sandpaper. Knock out irregularities and high spots. Gently "feather" lumps where panels overlap.

When smooth, roll on a coat of resin. This should obliterate any pinholes where the resin didn't penetrate earlier.

If you wish, you can give the interior still another coat of resin, but it isn't necessary. In fact, you could even add more panels of cloth. Do so only if durability and strength are your overriding concerns. For normal use, you have more than enough cloth inside and outside. Each layer you add beyond this point will add up to 10 pounds of weight—and a great feature of this boat, aside from its beauty, is its lightness. Five layers below the water (3 outside, 2 inside) and two layers above water (1 outside, 1 inside) is all the fiberglassing it takes.

So, fellow builders, that's all there is to building and fiberglassing the hull. You've built the basic boat; a few finishing touches are all that remain.

At this point, you're ready to put the finishing touches on your boat—and so long as you stay within basic design guidelines, you now can really put your individual stamp on the Cosine Wherry. What we describe in this section is how *we* built the interior, but there are a number of variations possible which we'll describe. The approach we use is probably the easiest, but don't be afraid to try something a little different. Not every detail in the plans is engraved in stone. The dimensions, molds, shape, and freeboard specifications are worth following exactly, but seat position and height, for example, can be slightly altered for your comfort. With decorative details, you can take an even freer hand.

We fashioned the interior from spruce because spruce is lightweight. Other woods will work for both the hull and the interior, but the lighter the materials, the better the performance. And heavier is not always stronger. Passengers and rowers can bring aboard all the "carry" weight you need. The Cosine Wherry tracks best with 300 to 400 pounds of displacement, including the weight of living bodies, so there's no need to put much over a hundred pounds into wood, glass, epoxy, and fastenings.

We'll show you how we built the interior of our boat from the plans and point out some of the options you can try as you finish up.

the sheer are usually called gunwales or gunnels—but those terms are technically misnomers, descendants of a time when ships were equipped with guns and required a lower "rail" to keep them in place. The Cosine Wherry isn't designed to take cannon aboard. Even if it were, the gunnels would not run along the "top edge" of the boat, but would run further down where the cannon doors would open in the hull. Gunwales were merely rails designed to keep the guns from pitching out. So on the Cosine Wherry we call the gunwales the guards.

The guards provide an elegant trim and a chance for you to exercise some creativity. The outer guard, naturally, runs along the outside of the hull; the inner guard, on the inside of the boat. The two are held together by blocks. The blocks aren't necessary; the inner guard and outer guard can be glued to the hull rather than to blocks (with a strip glued to both as a trim cap). But the spacing blocks are attractive—and useful, too. With blocks between guards, it's easier to pick up the boat. When you turn the boat over, the spacing blocks act as vents so water can drain out.

The blocks also act to strengthen the guards themselves. And the spaces between blocks are handy spots to tie on fenders or landing lines, making cleats unnecessary.

Materials

4 - ¾" x 1" x 16' pieces of spruce   (for guards)
Lumber for seats
Eye bolt
Oarlock hardware
Epoxy glue
Screws
19' rub shoe
Elastomeric bedding compound
High density urethane foam (about 2-2½ cu. ft.)
High gloss marine varnish
Paint or varnish thinner
Satin marine varnish

Guards

The first piece of this final puzzle provides protection as well as beauty. The inner and outer guards running along

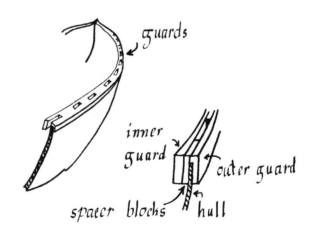

Guards and spacer blocks.

Install Outer Guards

The guard material we chose was spruce, ¾" x 1" (actual dimensions), about 16' long. Using a table saw, we cut a rabbet lengthwise, so that from each outer guard we removed a 16' x ¾" section.

This notching enabled us to fit the guard neatly over the edge of the hull, eliminating the need to add an additional strip as a cap.

If you don't have the machinery for rabbeting, don't panic. A cap works well, too. It just requires more gluing.

Allowing the outer guard strip to go past both stem and stern, glue it on with a stiff mixture of epoxy, clamping just as you did for the planking. Glue and clamp both outer guards and wait for them to take hold .

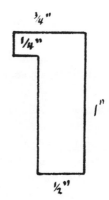

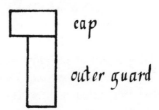

Cross section of two different versions of outer guards.

Clamping and gluing the outer guard to the hull.

Measure for Thwarts

Before installing your blocks and inner guards, it's wise to do a little layout, marking where the seats and oarlocks will be placed. You can also plan where to place each block.

Symmetry is elusive. Your feet may not be precisely the same size, and the two sides of our faces don't match perfectly (or so portrait photographers tell us). Likewise, the left side of the hull is not an exact mirror image of the right side of the hull. If you measure both sides stem to the transom, you may find one side longer than the other. (It will be close, of course, close enough to fool the eye.) Thus, when we locate the seats, we don't want just to measure an equal distance along each side; by the time we get to the end, we can be an inch or more off, meaning the seats won't appear "square" in the boat.

To restore a semblance of symmetry, then, we began by stretching a centerline string, tacked from the stem to the middle of the transom. Using a straight batten of wood long enough to reach from side to side (we call this a "how-far stick"), we marked the center point for the three seats (thwarts). Since the center string is above the "how-far stick," we used a square to bring our thwart points down to the stick. The exact location of each seat is indicated on the plans (where distances refer to measurements on the center string). Finally, to assure that our stick was perpendicular (90°) to the center string, we stretched a wire from the stem to each end of the "how-far stick." The length of the wire was calculated using the Pythagorean Theorem: the square of the hypotenuse is equal to the sum of the squares of the sides in a right (90 degree) triangle. If this geometry baffles you, use a square to assure that your "how-far stick" is at right angles to the center string.

Mark the thwart positions on both sides of the hull and your basic layout is done.

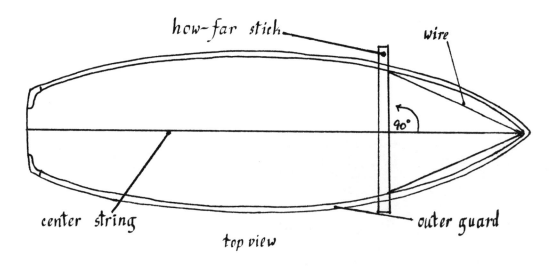

One method of laying out the thwarts perpendicular to the centerline of the boat. Note: If the two wires are of equal length, the how-far stick must be perpendicular to the centerline.

Squaring up the thwart positions with wires.

Picking the distance off the center string for thwart locations.

Cut and Install Blocks

Now cut blocks from the same material as the guards. There are two kinds of blocks: those for oarlock pads (optional— not shown in plans) and those for intermediate support. The oarlock pad blocks (three on each side) are longer than the intermediate blocks. The lengths we used are on the plans. The blocks will be "sandwiched" neatly between the inner and outer guards.

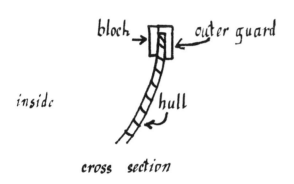

Cross section of outer guard and spacer block.

Install the oarlock pad blocks first, three on each side, *always aft (toward the transom)* of the marks you just made for seats (thwarts). Check plans to see exactly how far aft. Then use the old reliable glue and clamp method, making sure that the oarlock pad blocks flow fairly smoothly into the outer guard.

Once you have the oarlock pad blocks in place, three on each side, you can locate all the intermediate blocks. *The space between all blocks should be equal*, even if the length of blocks varies. Nevertheless, we admit that it is no great disaster even if the blocks aren't spaced evenly—it just looks better to the finicky eye. Measure off the distances between oarlock pad blocks and calculate where you want to place the other blocks. When you're satisfied with your layout, glue and clamp all the blocks *except those blocks which are aft of the back oarlock pads* toward the transom.

Gluing spacer blocks to the rail.

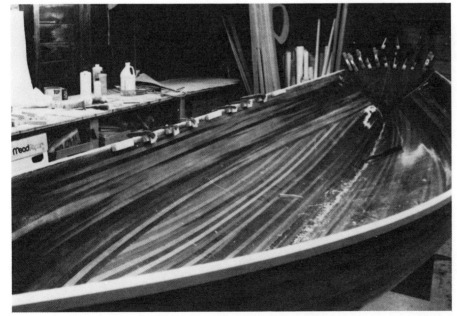

At this point, we can (if we wish) give our trim a professional turn. At the transom, the lines of the boat "flair" or twist dramatically. We emphasized this graceful curve by beveling the blocks in this section to conform to that pleasing shape. We beveled the block nearest the transom and glued it in.

An even fancier (and much more time-consuming) method is to taper both ends of the guard about 20%. This taper is cut in all four sides of the guard, so that it becomes less wide *and* less thick as it reaches stem and stern.

These "grace notes" will make your boat appear more slender and less bulky; they do not make for better performance, increased strength, or anything remotely practical. If you want aesthetic improvements, however, this is one way to go. It just takes more time.

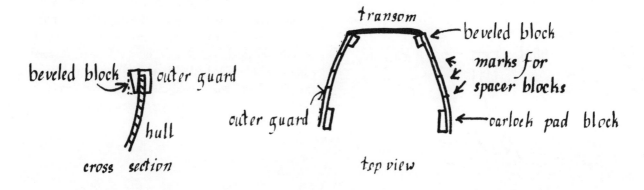

Gluing the spacer blocks to the hull. Note that all the spacer blocks aft of the oarlock pad have some bevel. The spacer block at the transom has the most bevel, about half the thickness of the block.

Make the spacer block at the transom first.

Install Inner Guard and Transom Cap

Once all your blocks except the tapered ones are in place, it's time to finish the sandwich. The inner guard is installed against the blocks just as the outer guard was against the hull—with glue and clamps, of course. Glue the inner guard in place and then insert your beveled blocks, checking that they conform to the curve of the inner guard. When you have these blocks beveled to your satisfaction, glue them to the inner hull and inner guard surfaces.

TIP: The joint of the guards—where left guard meets right guard inside and out at the stem—can be a difficult fit and will require some careful trimming with a knife or saw. There are some tricks of the trade, but if your carpentry skills desert you at this juncture, try creating that joint on both forward ends before you glue in the guards. If you make a mistake, you can try again, losing only an inch or so off one end of each guard. The best method is to copy the angle for the cut from the plans and try it out—do the two guards really join at the stem tightly? Then shape the ends from there with a block plane.

Last, cut and glue and screw into place a strip from the guard material to fit over the transom. This caps everything off.

Your guards are up, and, best of all, you've finished the most difficult phase of the interior work.

Inner guard and blocks glued in as far back as the aft oarlock pad.

Getting ready to install beveled blocks aft of the aft oarlock pad.

Seats (Thwarts)

You may spend some time standing in this boat, but you'll want to sit down, too (especially when rowing). The Cosine Wherry is designed for up to five sturdy seats (or thwarts, as they are also called), but we eliminated the front seat, wanting to use this space for storage while at sea.

You've already used the "how-far stick" to mark the recommended position for each seat. You now have some leeway in positioning the seats. The plans tell you how far down on the inner hull to place the seat supports, but if you're extremely tall or short, you can lower or raise the "riser marks" for comfort.

There are plenty of comfort and use options at this stage. For example, you can support the seats on each side with a riser system or with individual blocks. We decided to use risers. A riser is simply a continuous strip of wood running from the front seat to the rear seat on each side (and it may be a little stronger than individual blocks under each seat). Whichever method you use, installation is the same: glue the support system to the inside of the hull at the proper locations and then screw into the support from the *outside* of the hull.

The risers must be firmly attached, and screw and glue is the best method. The seats will help prevent the hull itself from distorting during use—provided the seats are securely

supported. When you've placed your screws through the hull into the supports, putty over the heads. (Yes, the screws do "break" the fiberglass on the outside, but the putty provides protection, and the screws go in well above the waterline.)

Once your risers are secure, cut out the seats to fit.

The three center seats require seat posts in the middle to withstand their all-too-human load. The plans call for wooden cleats to fasten the posts to the bottom of the hull and the seats. Sequence is crucial here. First, position the center seat and screw it into place on the risers. Carefully

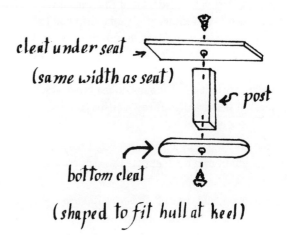

cleat under seat →
(same width as seat)
← post
bottom cleat
(shaped to fit hull at keel)

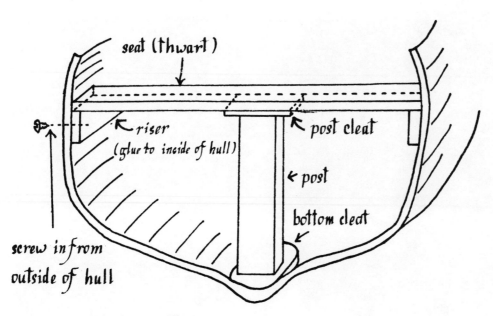

A cross section of the thwart installation.

seat (thwart)
← riser
(glue to inside of hull)
post cleat
← post
bottom cleat
screw in from outside of hull

measure the distance from the underside of the seat to the center of the bottom of the boat (the keel). Cut a batten of that length and try it under the seat. Then construct a seat post with cleats on each end that will fit under the seat. Posts can be cut from 1½″ x 1½″ material. (Actually, we used table legs and they worked fine.) Round and bevel to fit a wooden cleat for the bottom of the boat; cut a cleat the exact width of the seat to attach under the thwart. Glue and screw the cleats into the ends of the seat post, checking the overall length against your measured batten. Finally, unscrew the seat, slide the post into position, screw the seat down as a final check, then glue everything (cleats, seat, risers) in position. Now screw the seat into place for the last time. A snugger job was never done. Repeat this process with the other two center seats. (When you decide to install the fourth or the fifth seat, no posts will be needed.)

Quarter Knees, Breast Hook, Deck, Bow Eye, Oarlock Sockets (and Other Visible Means of Support)

Once the seats are in, you must add yet more bracing. (Why not? You've come this far, and your boat might as well last a lifetime.)

Bracing at the rear is provided by the quarter knees. These are shaped to fit into both corners of the transom. Copy the shape from the plans. We used spruce lumber.

The quarter knees must be installed in the same strong way as the risers were. (That is: glue to the inside of the hull and transom, then screw in from the outside of the hull. And remember: putty or plug over the screw heads.)

The breast hook is a similar brace installed to give the stem added strength. The shape and position of the breast hook you'll find in the plans. One option here is to replace the breast hook with a small deck. We tried this, thinking it was easier to do than the breast hook. Well, it wasn't easier, but you can build a deck at this point.

Another option is a bow eye. A bow eye on the stem is handy if you want to tow the Cosine Wherry. To install a bow eye, you'll need to cut and shape a block and glue it to the inside of the stem. Then drill a hole through the stem and the backing block, and install the eye bolt in the hole with plenty of marine sealant.

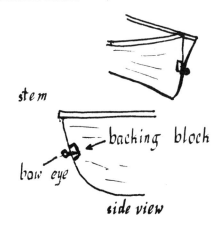

Suggested positioning of the bow eye.

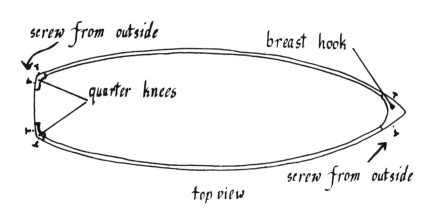

Location of the quarter knees, breast hook and screws.

Quarter knees installed. Note the open corners.

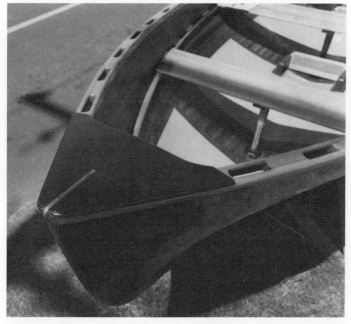

A small foredeck installed in place of a breast hook.

Now is also a good time to install the oarlock sockets. This is a simple matter of drilling a hole all the way through the center of each oarlock pad block, inserting the hardware, and gluing and screwing it into place. We made a modification here. We wanted to raise the oarlock sockets an inch-and-a-half for rowing comfort, so we first glued a new pad in place over the oarlock pad block. (We then drilled all the way through both pads, which makes it possible for water to drain through.)

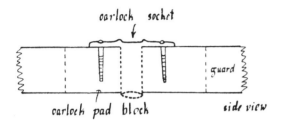

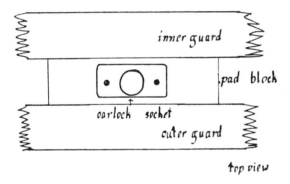

One type of oarlock socket installation.

Rub Shoe

Some weeks and pages ago, we mentioned that a metal rub shoe would one day be installed on the keel. The day has come. The shoe piece acts as a buffer, something to take the shock when the boat is set on shore or launching strip (or accidentally scrapes bottom). It should run over and down the stem, all along the keel line of the hull and up a few inches past the skeg.

The rub shoe is a ½" or ⅜" half-oval continuous strip of brass, bronze, or (if the boat is usually in fresh water) aluminum. Total length is about 19 feet. It helps if this piece is predrilled every 3" or so. The crucial task in installing the rub shoe is bedding. The piece must be completely bedded in an urethane elastomeric bedding compound (such as Sika-Flex or 3M 5200) to form a water-tight seal between the shoe and the hull. (Avoid at whatever cost bedding compounds with silicone or asphalt bases, as well as the caulks advertised for use with bathtubs and home plumbing.)

Apply the bedding compound, then screw the shoe in place. Number 4, ¾" oval-head screws of brass, bronze, or stainless steel will work. Have a coarse cloth and paint thinner at hand and clean up any residue of bedding compound IMMEDIATELY. (You can also attach a shoe to the top of the transom in the very same way. This helps protect the boat when it is set on a hard surface upside down.)

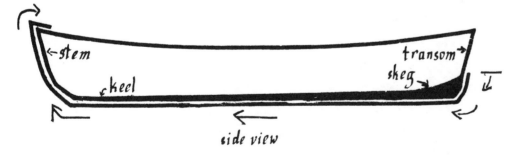

When putting on the brass rub shoe, start at the stern and work forward.

Footing and Flotation

Foot braces or stretchers — 2 ″ x 2 ″ lengths of spruce glued to the bottom of the boat — act as wonderful points for leverage when you row. They aren't necessary, but they are handy, and you can position them exactly where they feel best to you.

Other footing options include wooden floorboard slats (¼ ″ x 2 ″ spruce sections) glued in to prevent feet from slipping, and nonskid tape, available commercially, which you simply tape down to increase your traction. (The nonskid tape lasts a few seasons.)

Installing 2 to 2 ½ cubic feet of high density urethane foam under the seats is recommended for safety. It can be glued in place and does not need to be covered. (If the boat pitches and turns over in bad weather, the flotation helps make turning the boat upright easier.) The flotation is distributed in three equal portions, a third under the forward seat, a third under the back seat, and a third under both sides of the center seat. Before installing the flotation, however, it is best to sand and varnish the interior.

*Adjustable stretcher showing **nonskid tape** and cut-out for post. There are several variations for stretchers that work well.*

*Inside finished, including stretchers and **nonskid** paint.*

Sanding and Varnish

Sand your interior work, rounding or beveling the edges according to the plans. When everything is smooth and shapely, apply two coats of varnish and thinner (one part thinner to three parts high-gloss exterior or marine varnish) to the spruce work—to seats, risers, guards, blocks, quarter knees, breast hook (or deck). Sand between coats. Then apply two more coats of varnish.

Next, lightly sand back the hull—the entire hull, meaning inside and outside—and apply two coats of *satin* exterior or marine varnish to all inside hull areas. (A high-gloss varnish on the hull inside would create too much glare.) Next apply two coats of high-gloss exterior varnish to the outside of the hull, and one final coat to the woodwork. Note that the varnish you select must have ultraviolet filtering (to protect the epoxy from ultraviolet rays).

Many boatbuilders paint the bottom with two coats of marine or bottom paint (from the waterline down). At the waterline, they mask off a line and paint a trim stripe. Bottom paint isn't necessary, but many people prefer it; they complain that without it, the varnished boat looks like a piano.

Obviously, all matters of decorative painting are up to you. You can, for example, paint the inside, too.

Variations

Our instructions and plans are meant as suggestions—as the easiest way to build a sound, superior rowboat. While the dimensions and mold sections are fixed, the choice of materials, of interior work, and of painting are up to you. We've described how we did it, and it worked; but we hope you'll also add your own variations. (One variation we are skeptical about, however, is conversion to sail. The Cosine Wherry could be made to sail, but this would seriously compromise its performance as a rowboat. If you want to build a fine sailing-rowing combination, contact us; we have other designs better suited to your requirements.)

So there you are. You're finished. No more steps. Absolutely none. Your Cosine Wherry is ready to row wherever you want to take it, from lake to sea, in fair weather or foul. But no matter where you go, let us know how you do.

Unless you live on lakefront, river bank, or priceless ocean coast, you'll be driving your new boat to water. And here's where you'll appreciate the light weight of the Cosine Wherry. A wife and her husband, a parent and child, or even one adult who has practiced a few times can easily place the boat upside down on car rack. The maneuver is far more a matter of balance than of strength.

Since the spruce gunnels are soft, you'll want pads on your rack bars. Ropes from the bow and stern to your car bumpers are a good idea.

The only thing to remember about all this is that you must tie the boat to the car rack. One of our crew who shall remain nameless forgot this; as he drove off, he saw in his rear view mirror a new Cosine Wherry sailing backwards down the highway. The boat was not damaged in the least, by the way. It made it to the water that very day, in far better shape than its distressed owner.

You won't need a trailer for your Cosine Wherry. It will ride nicely on about any car roof rack.

It is our fond hope that rowing might soon sweep the nation, as jogging has done recently. Frankly, we see no good reason why it shouldn't. Rowing is less jolting to the body than jogging, more pleasurable we think, and quite invigorating. Rowing is good exercise at any age. It's an Olympic sport, too, and the tradition of rowing is far older and richer than of marathon running. A row on a lake, river, or bay soothes the mind and spirit. And on a summer day, there's nothing grander, especially when you're in a rowboat which tracks and glides as a real rowing vessel should.

To enjoy rowing to the fullest, you need suitable oars. Oars of spruce befit your boat's classy looks and performance. Spruce, like the Cosine Wherry rowboat, is light and efficient. A nine foot length is right for the oars—and spoon blades are the best. Unfortunately, spoon blades cost nearly three times what flat blades do. But you can whittle flat blades into more spoon-like shapes yourself. (Most flat blade oars are too heavy for comfortable rowing anyway.)

It is nice to have two sets of oars because this boat is a joy to row in tandem.

One more note on oars: they wear in the oarlocks. Oars should be fitted with leathers and buttons, or stops. The new plastic ones work well, but rubber "leathers" tend not to stay in place. Plastic "leathers" are heat shrunk onto the loom of the oar. Genuine leather may be laced on or glued in place with contact cement.

The Cosine Wherry moves best when the waterline on the hull rides parallel to the water surface. The positions of rowers and passengers therefore has a direct influence on how your rowboat rides. When you row alone without passengers, sit at the center facing back. But suppose you have passengers or two rowers? Where does everyone sit for maximum performance?

The general rule is to distribute weight evenly; when this is not possible, shift heavier persons to the rear. There is more displacement aft, so that's where the load goes. It is also difficult to row with a passenger on the center seat. So arrange rowers and passengers with the weight equally distributed or, when necessary, with the heavier load nearer the transom.

The Cosine Wherry reaches optimum design position in saltwater with two 200-pound rowers and no gear. But you can certainly take on more passengers. We've rowed with four people aboard quite comfortably.

One thing we've discovered is that to maintain harmony one set of oars is plenty when there are more than two people aboard. Two sets of oars churning away with passengers about quickly carries you to the shores of bedlam.

The other thing we've discovered is that this rowboat is a joy to use. We think you'll make this same discovery for yourself every time out.

Rowing the Cosine Wherry is an activity that can bring pleasure and health benefits the year round.

Oar Construction

The following drawings outline the construction of an oar designed by Rich Kolin and used by Saint Francis Rowing Club as a training oar. The dimensions given are in feet, inches and eighths. The handle, loom and blade center are made from 1-⅞" square by 8' long Sitka spruce stock. The blade sides are made from 1-⅞" square by 2' long Sitka spruce stock. The stock pieces are glued together with urea resin or epoxy and then shaped as indicated in the drawings. The blade tip is made from Honduran mahogany or a similar hardwood. Full scale plans are available from Flounder Bay Boat Lumber.

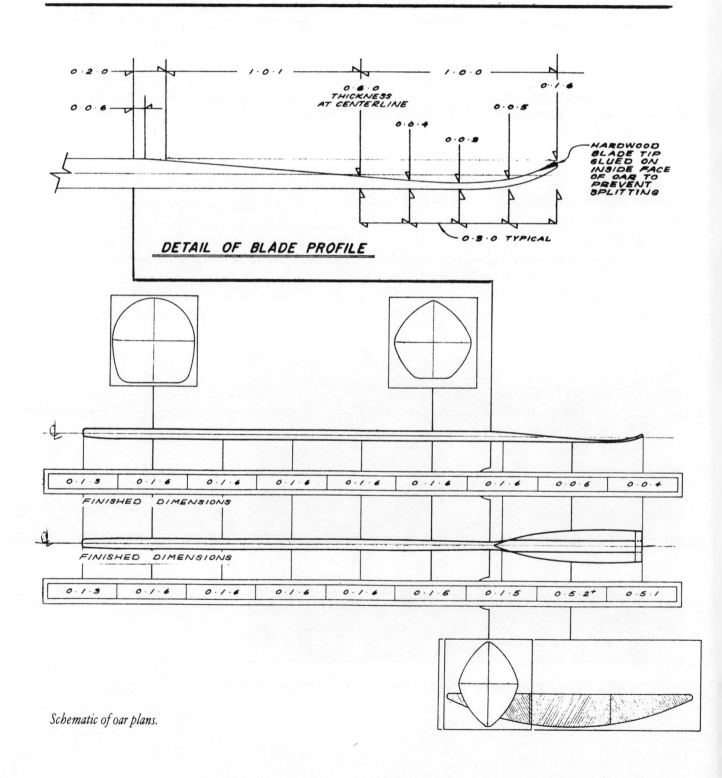

Schematic of oar plans.

Ripping Strips

Flounder Bay Boat Lumber can provide you with pre-cut wooden strips, ready to glue and fiberglass. But if you have time and want to save some money, you can rip your own strips.

Any yard handling premium grades of marine lumber should be able to supply you with the raw materials for strips (1" x 6" x 16' boards of western red cedar, redwood, northern white cedar, sitka spruce, southern pine, or eastern white pine). Just be sure the wood is light, strong, and clear. Rot resistance is no problem because the wood will be sheathed in fiberglass.

You'll need to rip slightly over one hundred 16-foot-long strips. Select the clearest grade possible (sometimes called "C or better") and always ask for flat grain material. How much material should you buy? The answer depends on how the yard mills the lumber. For example, we supply boards about 6" wide, planed to 3/4", and labeled S2S (meaning surfaced on two sides). The normal lumber yard can supply you with similar boards, but they are only 5½" wide and are labeled S4S (meaning surfaced on four sides). The width is important in ordering. Figure on buying nine 1 x 6 x 16' clear, flat grain boards from normal lumber yard stock (where a 1 x 6 is actually only 5½" wide). If you buy true 1 x 6 material, you'll only need seven 16" boards.

A common nominal 1 x 6 board will yield about 12 strips for your boat, while a true 1 x 6 board (a full 6" wide) will yield about 14 strips.

Even when you specify clear lumber, you may find a knot or two near the end or on one side. This is not a catastrophe. Nearly half the strips you need will be less than the full 16' length, allowing you to cut the knots out. If you get to the end of the stripping operation and find that you need to put a couple of shorter strips together to make a longer one, don't worry. Just butt the two strips together and apply wood glue at the joint.

A final caution in picking out strip plank material: There is a lot of wood on the market today called finish stock—and sometimes the back side is rough. Don't try it. The boards you want must be smooth on both sides.

Once you have the raw stock, you can set up a table saw (or band saw) to rip strips.

If you use a table saw, be sure it is at least a 7½", 1-horsepower model. Anything less is probably too small for this job. A square gullet ripping blade is fastest; it gives a rough finish, but is acceptable. A combination blade will also work, but it's slower. A carbide tooth blade is best of all and less frustrating to use than a steel blade. If you already have a good steel blade, it may not be worth buying a carbide blade just to rip strips; but then be prepared to "point-up" your steel blade and clean off deposits of pitch and gum in the middle of the operation.

To rip easily and accurately, a few jig guides help. Station a few guides (wooden blocks) to hold the board you are cutting against the fence to prevent kickback. Attach another guide to the fence to hold the wood down. Since you're sawing long strips, it's handy to have in-feed support (a sawhorse or table so that you're not supporting 16' of board in thin air) and off-feed support (to help the board come off the table saw without raising up). Feed supports will contain the spread of frustration. Having a friend around to help with the long end of the board is one of the best "sawhorses" going.

By the way, much is made of the difference between the saw kerf taken by a band saw and by a table saw. It is true that a table saw usually takes at least a 3/32" bite, often closer to a 1/8" bite, while the band saw takes only a 1/16" kerf. The band saw appears to be the economical choice. But it is hard to rip in a straight line using the band saw. You need a good long fence, jig guides to hold the board against the fence, and a brand new blade with a minimum width of ½" (¾" is better). The tooth pattern should not exceed seven to the inch (five to the inch is better). Even with the right blade and set up, however, cutting straight is difficult. The sharpest blade has a tendency to wander. Once the blade hits anything that knocks the points off, you will have to stop and sharpen it before you can cut true.

So, if you rip strips with a band saw, have a spare blade or two on hand. And no matter what saw you use, wear protective goggles or a full face mask, along with ear plugs. Saws are dangerous and noisy.

Ripping strips is not that time-consuming. If everything goes right, you'll spend about three hours at the saw. Since nothing ever goes that right, of course, expect to spend at least six hours on this task. When you rip your own strips, you save about a third on the cost of wooden planks for the hull.

About Resins

We recommend epoxy resins, not polyester resins, when we fiberglass boats at our shop. One reason is that a sealer coat is required to make a polyester resin stick to wood. Polyester resin simply will not cure in the presence of oxygen or oil, and wood can be oily or porous (trapping air). That's the chemistry of the beast. The same is not true of epoxy resins. They set up even when exposed to air and wood oil, and they do not require a sealer coat.

Epoxy resins which are specially formulated for marine use are also much less brittle over the long run than polyester resins, especially when applied at low temperatures with a great deal of catalyst. Polyesters—and most of the materials used to thin and clean them—are flammable: the catalyst is an oxidizing agent; and the fumes are toxic. Polyester resins also eat up gloves. You must use good (expensive) neoprene gloves. And it takes reams of sandpaper to sand between the stubborn coats of a polyester resin.

After handing down these harsh indictments, we have to admit that there are reasons to use polyester resins. You must decide if the advantages override the disadvantages.

Polyester resins are cheaper than epoxies—a third to half the cost. Polyesters are more widely available. The pot life of polyesters can be varied and controlled easily. Finally, polyester resins do wet out fiberglass cloth better than epoxy resins and give a slightly more brilliant finish.

We still prefer the epoxies. Here's why. Epoxy resins are not flammable, the fumes are relatively non-toxic, and usually they do not contain solvents. Epoxies are quite flexible and resist splitting, checking, and cracking. They adhere easily to wood (no wood sealers required). Adding hardener is easy. With polyester resins, you must count each drop of hardener you add; with epoxy resins, it is a simple general proportion, such as two or three to one.

Anyone who has worked with resins knows that the pot life (the time you have to use the resin once the hardener is mixed in) is an important consideration. The pot life of a polyester resin is regulated simply by changing the proportion of hardener. Some epoxy resins can not be so easily regulated. The most advanced marine epoxy resins, however, now come with several hardener systems; this allows us to tailor the pot life of epoxy to almost any task.

One thing to remember, especially if you work outside, in a carport, or anywhere that might be damp or cool, is to select a moisture-protective hardener for your resin. Epoxies are unsurpassed in the protection they offer against moisture. We were able to use one epoxy resin (Cold Cure) to laminate bent wooden ribs as they came hot and dripping wet straight from a steam box. We don't know if the manufacturer recommends this, but it worked fine. A resin that was not moisture-protected would have failed under such steamy conditions.

We recently used another epoxy resin (System Three) to ready a boat for one of Seattle's boat shows. We were sheathing at temperatures below freezing. It was rather damp, too. The epoxy worked fine, but the manufacturer still shudders when we describe the conditions of our success. Some epoxy resins, by the way, claim that they can be used under water, but we have not tested this ourselves.

Epoxy resins wet out (penetrate and saturate) fiberglass cloth quite well, but polyester resins do an even better job. (Epoxies do a poor job when applied to heavy reinforcing fabrics with mat or thick roving, but these materials are not used on lightweight craft such as the wherry.) The final result on your boat, if you use epoxy, will be more than satisfactory. If you came upon two boats sitting side by side, one sheathed in polyester resin, the other in epoxy, you could probably tell the difference in clarity. If the boats were then separated by fifteen feet, no one could detect a difference in their finishes.

We've found that the epoxy resins have many advantages. The major disadvantage, of course, is the higher cost; but we believe it's worth paying.

Fiberglass Cloth

For the fourteen-foot wherry, we used 6-ounce, 60-inch, volan-finish cloth. Other widths will work, but your layout pattern will then differ from what we describe in this book. Four-ounce cloth can be used if reduced weight is a vital consideration; and one layer of cloth can be eliminated safely from the bottom. There's probably no advantage to getting the boat down below 80 pounds; its performance would then be compromised.

Avoid bargain cloth, especially when it comes from military or industrial surplus stores. The danger with cheaper materials is that the volan finish may have been damaged. The strength of the cloth is lessened if the fibers are allowed to rub and scratch each other, so the finish must be properly manufactured and the cloth carefully shipped and stored. We have tested samples of cloth where the strength varied as much as 50% in a single piece. Since this cloth imparts tensile strength to the boat, weak spots can not be tolerated. Use the best quality cloth you can buy. This might seem unnecessarily expensive, but it's cheaper than having your boat come apart.

Materials

Let's be specific about the materials we used to develop the wherry. The cloth was a Dow Corning volan-finish material. The epoxy resins were System Three[1], Cold Cure[2], and Sun Cure[2]. We also used Five Cure[2] epoxy glue.

We chose System Three epoxy resin because it was economical and moisture-protected. It also has a variable pot life, good wet out and clarity, and works under a wide range of temperature and humidity conditions. System Three's two-to-one hardener mixture is convenient, and we found the factory service excellent. We have used Cold Cure for years. It has the same fine features as System Three, but it may not wet out quite as easily and is more expensive. The manufacturer claims that Cold Cure produces a stronger sheath.

System Three is a good, modern boatbuilder's epoxy.
It works with any of three hardeners (hence its name)—the fast, the medium, or the slow (1, 2, or 3). For the Pacific Northwest and other damp, cool areas, we recommend the fast hardener. When temperatures reach the 70° and 80° range, the medium hardener is best. For you sunbelters (90°+), the slow hardener or a mixture of the slow and medium hardeners will produce the right pot life.

Sun Cure is a brilliant, clear resin with a fast wet out. It is perhaps the strongest resin around, a joy to use because of its long pot life, and about the same cost as Cold Cure. The only drawback is that Sun Cure is not moisture-protected, so it should not be used unless you have a warm, dry, 70° shop. In the right work place, Sun Cure is the best epoxy resin you'll ever use, provided you can stand its long cure time (48 hours).

Five Cure is a five-minute epoxy glue that we rely on when we want a quick, strong bond. It is expensive, not truly waterproof, and somewhat brittle, but it is unsurpassed as a spot adhesive. Mixed with a little fine sawdust, Five Cure also becomes one of the finest wood putties ever.

There are other good epoxy resins on the market, but we chose these because they work reliably in lower temperatures and higher humidities. They also offer moisture protection. This is vital. If your resin does not harden in a reasonable time, you may have moisture in it, and then the only answer is sandpaper. If you use System Three or Cold Cure, you'll never have to start over. If you do start with a moisture-sensitive resin and the weather suddenly turns cool and damp, you can switch to a moisture-protected resin. We know of no common epoxy resin systems that are incompatible when cured.

Now for some final tips on the basic materials:

The cost of a low-temperature resin is usually less than the cost of installing a heating system or buying eight heat lamps.

When in doubt about sanding between coats, sand.

Avoid using surplus resins such as those originally blended for industry or the military. You have no way to tell how it will act in your shop. The closest thing to instructions you'll find is that the contents meet mil spec #4319846742322-H.

Stay with a reputable manufacturer and supplier. That way you have somebody to hammer on if something goes haywire.

Don't try to improve the epoxy by adding chemicals of your own design.

Remember that your manufacturer's representative is the person to ask if you have epoxy questions. Don't ask the people who bag your groceries or tune up your outboard.

Over the years, we have had some epoxy resin failures. Only in one case (when we used an off-brand) could we trace our failure to the product. In all other instances, we had pushed the epoxy past its performance limits—had not mixed it thoroughly enough, forgotten a key ingredient, or simply not measured accurately.

So follow instructions, use good materials, do it right, but don't forget to have some fun. A good boat is more than the sum of its materials.

[1] System Three is a trademark of System Three Resins, Inc.
[2] Cold Cure, Sun Cure and Five Cure are trademarks of Industrial Formulators, Inc.

The following is a list of all the materials you'll need to build a Cosine Wherry. Be sure to read the entire book before selecting any materials.

Wood:

approx. 100	¼" x ¾" x 16' strips of western red cedar*
¼ sheet	12mm marine plywood
2 sq. ft.	4mm marine plywood
22' lin.	½" x 10" spruce for thwarts
76' lin.	½" x 1" spruce for gunwales
10' lin.	1" x 2" spruce for seat risers
2' lin.	¾" x 6" spruce for skeg
4' lin.	1" x 8" spruce for knees
10' lin.	½" x 2" spruce for stretchers
4' lin.	1" x 3" mahogany for blocking & deck beam
3	12" posts for thwarts

Resins and Fiberglass:

2 gal.	epoxy resin
1 gal.	resin hardner
1 bag	phenolic microballoons or wood flour
25 yds.	60" glass cloth

Varnish, Tape, Brushes:

2 qts.	marine varnish with ultraviolet shield
1 qt.	marine topside enamel
1	small pack of nonskid compound
1 roll	striping tape
102'	4" tape
6	brushes
1	5" squeegee
1 roll	masking tape

Sandpaper:

6 sheets	40 grit sandpaper
4 strips	80 grit longboard
10 sheets	80 grit
4 sheets	120 grit
4 discs	80 grit

Glue:

1	large kit of 5 minute epoxy glue
30	sticks of hot-melt glue

Hardware:

20'	½" brass half oval
25	#12 x 2" silicon bronze wood screws
100	#6 x ⅝" oval head stainless steel screws
6	bronze oarlock sockets
4	bronze oarlocks

Materials for the mold are listed on page 9.

*Note: Not all of the strips need to be 16' long. If you're willing to deal with several lengths of wood the following combination of ¼" x ¾" strips will be enough wood to build this boat:

Strip length	Number of strips needed
15'	40
14'	24
12'	30

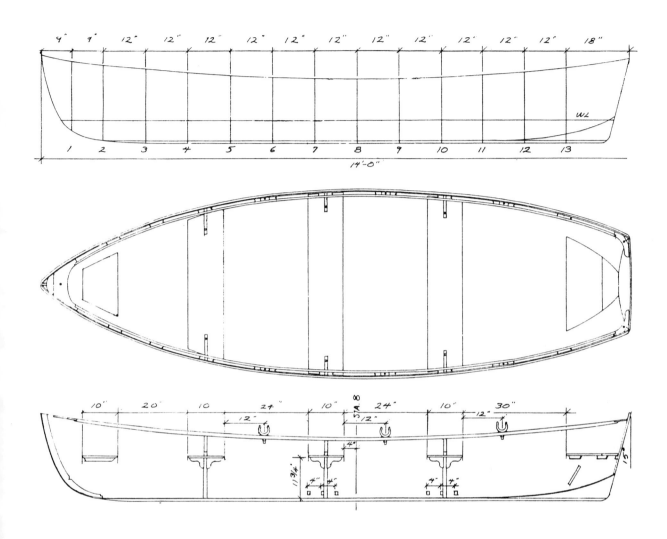

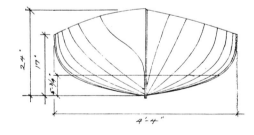

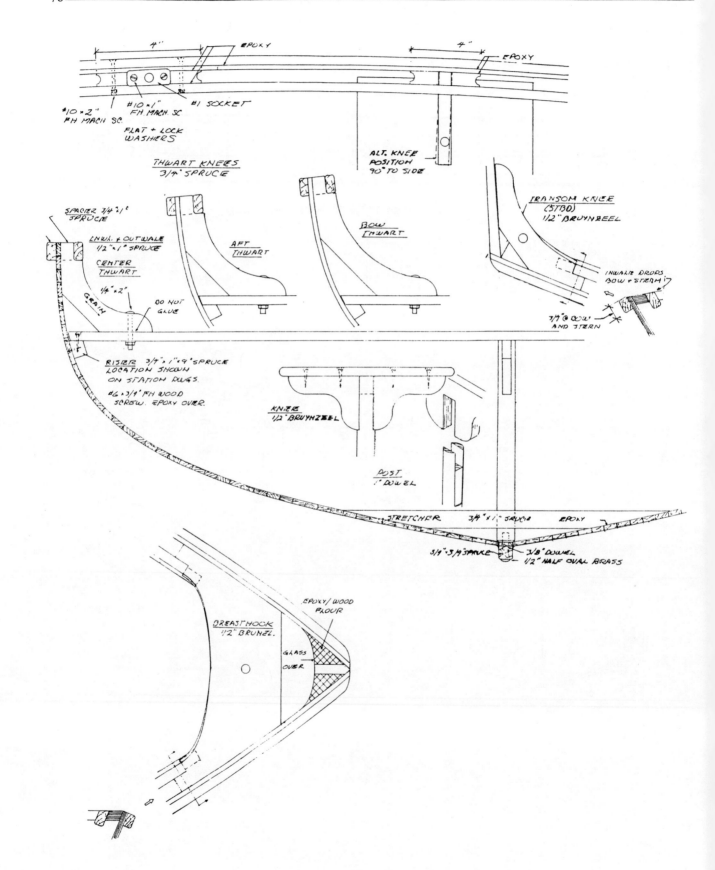

Glossary

baseline	The reference line from which many measurements of the boat are taken.
batten	A small, and usually long, flexible strip of wood.
breast hook	The triangular piece of wood that helps hold the two sides of the boat together at the bow.
Bruynzeel	A type of very fine marine plywood manufactured in Holland.
centerline	The reference line, running stem to stern, used to identify the exact middle of the boat.
cleat	A piece of wood used as reinforcement or used to attach one unit to another.
cove	Same as fillet.
epoxy hardener	A chemical compound which acts as a catalyst to speed the hardening of liquid epoxy resins.
fairing	The act of rendering a surface free from unevenness, irregularity or blemishes. In this context it is the application of putty and then sanding to make the surface of the boat sweet and smooth. It also applies to the adjustment of the station molds so that the planks will lay in a smooth and even curve.
fiberglassing	Sheathing the boat with glass fiber reinforcing cloth and saturating this cloth with a resin.
guard	The piece of wood that goes around the top edge of the boat to protect it from bumps.
gunwale	Another term for guard.
gusset	A reinforcing plate or brace.
inwale	A long strip of wood running along the top inside edge of the boat. The inwale adds strength to the boat.
jig	An armature or fixture used as a building aid. In this case the boat is built on a jig, or mold.
keel	The central bottom beam of the boat, running fore to aft, or lengthwise.
keel line	That line which describes the outside face of the keel.
knees	Reinforcing braces placed at corners, such as the transom knee, thwart knees, or quarter knee.
leathers	Leather sleeves placed on the oars to prevent the oarlocks from wearing on the oar shaft.
linen fiber	An agent made from chopped linen fiber that is added to resins to make a structural putty used for making fillets.
microballoons	An additive used with resins to make fairing putty fillers.
milled fiber	Finely chopped glass fiber used for building stronger fillets.
mold	An appliance used to control shape. This boat is built over a mold or jig.
outwale	Another term for guard.
rabbet	A relief, or notch, cut horizontally along the length of a piece of wood or timber.
rub shoe	The metal or wood strip that runs along the bottom of the keel to protect the bottom from scraping. The rub shoe is sometimes referred to as a rub strake.
scribing	Marking, or scoring, the wood with a pointed instrument.
sheerline	The top edge of the uppermost, full length, hull plank.

skeg	A small, fixed rudder attached to the aft end of the keel. The skeg helps the boat hold a straight course.
spokeshave	A type of plane originally used for shaping wheel spokes. It is either pushed or pulled with two hands and comes in a variety of shapes and sizes. In boatbuilding it is especially useful in oar and spar making.
squeegee	A tool, usually made of plastic or rubber, used for spreading resin.
station	A cross sectional form which represents the shape of the boat at a given point along the boat's length. (The full size patterns for each station are included in the plans.) When a number of stations are lined up, together they create a mold or jig which represents the shape of the entire boat.
stealer	A small, triangular shaped piece of planking used to alter the direction in which the full length planks are running.
stem	The piece of wood which forms the forward end of the boat. It connects to the keel and joins the two sides of the boat together.
stern	A general term used to refer to the aft, or back, end of a boat. The end of the boat opposite the stem.
stipple	To jab with a short stabbing motion.
stretchers	Braces attached to the bottom of the boat, against which you can put your feet while rowing.
strongback	A stable structure, or backbone, upon which the stations are aligned to form the mold or jig.
surform	A type of coarse wood rasp that comes in a variety of shapes.
thwarts	Seats
transition line	This line runs lengthwise along the boat at the point where bottom planks meet the top planks. This line, which is nearly coincident with the waterline, is the point at which the planking pattern changes.
transom	The piece of marine plywood that forms the back end of the boat.
waterline	The line, running lengthwise along the boat, which is defined by the water when the boat is floating and evenly loaded with its displacement load.
wood flour	A very fine, dry, wood dust usually collected at the big sanders at plywood mills.

Since this book was first published in 1985 many wherries have been built; quite a number of which received either guidance, and/or materials from Flounder Bay. We're delighted to report that the design and building techniques have stood the test of time. Except for some minor inconsistencies, there is little we have changed. There are, however, some additional topics we would like to address here: the use of bead and cove technique, a ladder frame, design variations.

Bead and Cove Strips

The bead and cove technique has been around for many years, though in the past it was generally used on planking of a larger dimension. When we built the first three prototype wherries we did not have the equipment to make beaded and coved strips. We now have the equipment to shape the edge of the strips—one edge is shaped convex, the other concave—and we now supply many builder's kits with the shaped strips. If you want to do the beading and coving yourself and you're lucky enough to have access to a shaper, you can order shaper blades for ¼″ strips. The other way to get the desired shape is with a router. Finding the right bits can be a challenge, however. The only source we know of is: Furnina Industrial Carbide, P.O. Box 308, Barry's Bay, Ontario, Canada K0J 1B0. What you need to order is a kit with ¼″ bead and cove routers and jig.

Cross section of bead & cove strips.

The beading and coving takes more time, of course, but the advantage is that the planking and fairing goes faster. The rounded edge of one strip fits into the concave edge of the adjacent strip. The other advantage, although purely cosmetic, is that this tighter fit prevents gaps that might allow light to show through the finished boat.

Where's the Waterline? Many builders prefer to cover the waterline with a broad boot-top, a paint stripe about 2-3 inches wide. In a boat built with square edged stips the waterline is generally just below the transition point, making it somewhat easy to find. The boot-top, in this case, usually covers both the waterline and the transition point. When you use bead and cove strips, which are more flexible, the transition point falls well below the waterline, hence it's a bit trickier to know where the waterline is. There are a couple of ways to solve this problem. First, you can mark the waterline on the molds as you are tracing the lines from the patterns. Then, when planking, transfer these points to the outside of the planks with a deep pin prick or a small nail hole, as the planks intersect the waterline points. A second method is to wait until the boat is finished, put it in the

water with a 200 pounder in the center seat, and mark enough points at the waterline so that you and a friend can lay out the entire line with a flexible batten, once the boat is out of the water.

Ladder Frame Strongback

Over the years we have used many different types of building jigs and strongbacks. The T-section strongback described in chapter two is easy and inexpensive to build, and hence is still the one of first choice for some builders. A ladder frame strongback offers some advantages over the T-section: it is more rigid, easier to fasten to and easier to support. However, it requires almost twice as much material, and takes more time to build, measuring, cutting and squaring. If you can afford the extra time and material, a ladder frame may be the way to go.

The drawing shows a typical ladder frame strongback with its rungs (running crosswise) fastened securely to the rails (running lengthwise) and each joint reinforced with a plywood gusset. You will want to make the frame longer than the building jig. For a 14′2″ boat, fifteen feet would be a good length. It should be a bit wider than a conventional ladder, approximately two and one half feet. The rungs are best spaced so they fall between the station molds, placing them in a good position to receive nails for the mold braces.

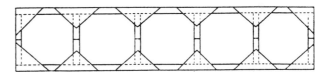

Top view of a typical ladder frame strongback.

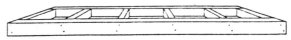

Side view of a typical ladder frame strongback.

Design Modifications

We have received a number of inquires regarding design modifications: from increasing the length to adding a sliding set or sail and dagger board. All of these modifications have been made and some plans are available at shops like ours which specialize in small boat construction. A note on changing the boat's length; there have been 16 and 21 foot versions built by stretching out the spaces between the stations, but no one has attempted to shorten it, and we suggest you don't try either. Before you get too brave about modification, remember that boat design is a function of use; if your primary goal is to sail, row faster or carry more weight than this boat was designed for, perhaps you should consider a different design.